About
BURT BRITTON
etc.

by Morris Lurie

About
BURT BRITTON
JOHN CHEEVER
GORDON LISH
WILLIAM SAROYAN
ISAAC B. SINGER
KURT VONNEGUT
and other matters
by
MORRIS LURIE

HORIZON PRESS ᗷL NEW YORK

Library of Congress Catalog Card No. 77-93936
ISBN 0-8180-1174-2 (cloth)
     0-8180-1175-0 (paper)

Printed in Australia by
Globe Press Pty. Ltd., Fitzroy.

Twelve of the pieces in this book originally appeared in *Nation Review*.

"Something Beautiful Is Going To Happen" originally appeared in *The Age*;

"Afternoon in Ossining" and "Vonnegut Lunch" in *Men in Vogue*;

"Anton Chekhov Addresses His Biographers," "Isaac Bashevis Singer, A Love Story," "An Open Letter To William Saroyan" and "Violence On Upper Broadway, New York City, USA" in *The National Times*;

"I'm Gonna Sit Right Down And Write Myself A Letter" in *The Daily Telegraph Magazine*;

"You Can Go Home Again" in *"Transatlantic Review"*;

"Portrait Of The Reader With A Million And A Half Books" utilizes material that originally appeared in *Nation Review, The National Times* and *Quadrant*.

But all of the pieces have been scrupulously rewritten, faultlessly restyled, in many instances copious enlargement has taken place, pleats added in the front, more room in the seat, rakish lines about the shoulders and leg . . . in short, a near-blinding elegance such as Henry James himself went practically bald striving so fruitlessly to attain.

It is my pleasure to acknowledge the assistance given to me by the Australian Council for the Arts during the writing of this book.

I should like to dedicate this book, with affection, with esteem, with ever-growing, dare I say it, practically love, to that essential essence, that blood-racing dynamo, that *force* of modern prose, Gordon Lish, late of *Esquire* magazine, but a small voice inside me says don't so I won't.

Instead, a whole gallery of fringe-friends comes gallumphing in, clamouring for recognition, and to them, ultimately, one must bow:

To Derrick Warren and David Hills and Max Robinson and Alan Lee and Clement Meadmore and Burt Britton,

To Mrs Wadman, who shelters me from the storm,

To a certain Rachelle, she of the mirrored ceiling,

To the great Dr Nameless, in more real life Graham King,

And (of course) to my gorgeous English model wife Caroline, without whose unstinting devotion at least two Nobel Prizes would have certainly accrued.

And to Miles Davis.

Contents

LITERARY MATTERS

Anton Chekhov Addresses His Biographers

My name is Anton Pavlovich Chekhov and I am seventy-three years dead. I breathed my last in the Hotel Sommer in the German spa of Badenweiler, near the Black Forest and the French border, attended by a Dr Schwörer and Olga, my devoted wife. I had been ill for a long time, many years, I was tired, weak, worn out. And bored. Oh, I was always bored. In the Hotel Sommer I suffered a heart attack. The good Dr Schwörer administered camphor injections and whiffs of oxygen. He also suggested I drink champagne. It was two o'clock in the morning, July 1, 1904. I looked at the doctor, I looked at my wife. *"Ich sterbe"* I said. Then I drained my glass of champagne, remarked to Olga that I hadn't drunk champagne for ages, turned onto my left side, and died. I was forty-four years old.

But a writer should be remembered, if he is remembered at all, not by such anecdotes, but by what he has written. I mean his published work, that which he chose to publish, and this is not the case with me. Not completely the case. I am weighed as much by my private writings as by those I designed for public print: my letters, some journals I kept, other notes. I am further invaded by the memoirs of others. But worse, much worse, are the biographies. A Life of Chekhov! A New Life of Chekhov! A Further Life of Chekhov! I have fallen into the domain of academics, scholars, "experts". I am endlessly analysed, dissected, gone over, probed. Why? What is there about my life that invites these scalpels? I am a writer, that's all.

Ah, but I wrote too much. God only knows how many words poured from my brain. Newly arrived in Moscow, my father a bankrupt — fled from Taganrog, that boring provincial town on the Black Sea where I was born, fled from his failed grocery store, his creditors howling, fled crouched under a mat in a cart in the dead of night — eight of us in two dismal damp rooms in the worst part of Moscow, I began to write.

I wrote like a fury. I wrote for copeks, for precious roubles. I was paid by the word, by the line, by the page. Sketches, lampoons, captions, jokes, the worst kind of humour, all manner of cheap rubbish, short, most of it, short and fast, rushed from my pen into the so-called comic papers of the day, *Splinters, The New Times, The Petersburg Gazette*, to support this family into which I had been born, my four brothers, my sister, my mother, my tyrannical talentless father.

While at the same time I studied to be a doctor.

My father found a job, drudge-work, poorly paid. My elder brothers Nicholas and Alexander (both far more talented than I, one an inspired artist, the other an insightful journalist) both took to drink, running up debts all over Moscow. Nicholas had tuberculosis, a disease which took him from us in his early twenties, before his life can be said to have properly begun, and though Alexander outlived me, he was, I fear, an alcoholic, whose sad life never amounted to anything.

Meanwhile, I wrote.

And things got better.

An esteemed writer named D V Grigorovich wrote to me. He said he was an avid reader of all my works. He said that I had "real talent . . . talent which sets you far above other writers of the younger generation." He said that I was destined to pen "truly artistic" works and would commit "a grievous moral sin" should I disappoint these high expectations. I thanked him, of course, I wrote to him at once, I was flattered and pleased, though I do think he laid it on with a trowel.

I began to publish in the Thick Journals, the serious literary magazines. I went to St Petersburg for the first time. I met all manner of important literary folk. I was praised, fussed over — which I didn't like much. Oh, how boring it is to be fussed over. Leave me in peace, please. But then I went to St Petersburg again, and again. I was always going to St Petersburg. The truth is, I quite liked the place. But then, I like all sorts of places. Do you know, one time I owned three houses in Yalta, and contem-

4

plated buying a fourth? I also owned a place in the country, at Melikhovo, fifty miles to the north of Moscow. Ah, there was a delightful place. A lovely old house, acres and acres of woods and gardens. I planted trees there, roses. How I loved to work in the garden at Melikhovo. And I wrote there too. I was always writing.

And I practiced medicine there too, tended to the peasants, wore myself thin with their ills. No, not for money, they had no money, and I wouldn't have taken it if they had. I did it because I wanted to, because it was my duty. I have always regarded medicine as my wife, literature as my mistress.

The days at Melikhovo, beautiful Melikhovo.

But there was something in me — how can I explain this? — that made me restless, always bored. Oh, I was bored. Bored in Moscow, bored in St Petersburg, bored in the country. Oh, the stifling provinces. And there were so many people coming to see me, taking up my time — or none. I don't know which was worse. I travelled. I went to Sakhalin, our Devil's Island, on the other side of Siberia. There was no train in those days, hardly a road. I slept in carts, on straw, in mud, rarely changed my clothes. I stank. I froze. I spat blood. I made a survey of the pitiful wretches imprisoned on that awful island, spoke to every single one. Yes, I published this. I think it is my finest work. If I am to be remembered, I hope it is for this.

I travelled. I was always travelling. I went to Berlin, Paris, Nice. Down the length of Italy. I sailed as far as Hong Kong. In Ceylon I made love to a black-eyed Indian girl in a coconut grove on a moonlit night.

Yes, I had affairs. Women seemed to find me attractive. They were always flitting around me, women and girls, but though I found this pleasant — as who wouldn't? — there was something inside me that said, Don't get too serious. Don't get involved. I don't mean that I am a cold fish, though sex has never been all that important to me, no, it's something else, I am not sure if I can make this clear. Women, I felt, wanted something of me, and I didn't feel in a position to give it. God knows, there was not much of me to begin with — what would there be if I gave *that* away?

My sister Mariya never married. Several times she came to me with suitors, for advice. I discouraged her. She never married. I think now that I was wrong.

5

But I married, married Olga Knipper, an actress with the Moscow Art Theatre, married in my forty-first year. You ask why? I search myself for reasons, a decent explanation. Oh, I loved Olga, of course, but was it just that? She had been my mistress, and now she was pressing me, urging . . . and I was tired, worn out. No, that's not right either, not the whole truth. I wanted, I think, an heir, a son. And Olga became pregnant, though the first I heard of it was when she told me that she had had a miscarriage. I was crushed before I had even had time to be elated.

Is there a God? Certainly there is irony, whichever way we turn.

I was tired, worn out. The Moscow Art Theatre had worn me out. Ah, Stanislavsky. How little he understood my plays. How he ranted, shedding emotions like a squeezed sponge. Didn't he see that I wanted my plays — *Uncle Vanya, The Cherry Orchard* — done quietly, matter-of-factly? What need is there of histrionics, all those theatrical gestures, those thundering climaxes and strutting walks? Life has drama enough when simply stated. Stanislavsky didn't understand this. None of them did.

Look at Gorky. He came to me for advice. I told him he should cultivate simple statements: "the sun set"; "it grew dark"; "it rained". I told him that if I wrote "The man sat on the grass" it is comprehensible because it is clear. Conversely, I am obscure, I tax the brain if I write "a tall, narrow-chested, ginger-bearded man of medium height sat down on the grass which was green and already crumpled by passersby; sat noiselessly, timidly and gazing about him fearfully." That doesn't go home at once, which is what fiction should do: straight away, in a second.

I wrote. I died. Now scholars dissect me, "experts" pick my bones, as though there was something in my boring life, some mystery, some trick, I don't know what they are looking for, but they feel they must find it. They categorize me, they pigeonhole me, they shuffle me about, try to make me fit their schemes. I am spoken of as the Sad-Eyed Poet of Twilight Russia; the Blazing-Eyed Prophet of Humanity's Glorious Future; the Wise Observer with a Wistful Smile and an Aching Heart; the Champion of the Little Man; The Gentle, Suffering Soul; the one who Loved People.

Please, please.

6

Many years ago I said a certain thing and now I should like to say it again, and that is all that I should like to say. *I am not a liberal. I am not a conservative. I am not an advocate of moderate reform. I am not a monk. Nor am I committed to non-commitment. I should like to be a free spirit, that's all.*

Isaac Bashevis Singer, A Love Story

"Certainly," said Herbert Gold, "you must see Singer." This was in San Francisco. We were having an evening together, the theatre, a marvellous Japanese meal. Gold wore a zip jacket, a shirt with flapped pockets, tight twill trousers tucked into paratrooper boots, a uniform of toughness, street fighter, city savvy, not quite right on a man of his age, mid to more forties, a grey grizzled beard. But slight, slim, a small man. Curious eyes. Dark. They switched on and off, one second couldn't-care-less, the next what's-going-on? Insecurity? Boredom? Bluff?

But Gold, as I told him over the phone, phoning him out of the blue, a visitor, a stranger, a Jewish writer from Australia he had certainly never heard of, turned me on to this craft or art or whatever you want to call it I practice, the writing of fiction, in particular, short stories. When I was seventeen or eighteen and didn't have the faintest idea what to do with my life, I stumbled on a story of his called *The Heart of the Artichoke*. "My father, his horny hands black with sulphur," it begins, "lit a cigar with a brief, modest, but spectacular one-handed gesture, his thumbnail crr-racking across the blue-headed kitchen match . . ." I had never read anything like it before, never seen such quicksilver prose. And then other stories. *The Burglars and the Boy. Susanna at the Beach. What's Become of your Creature? Love and Like.* I was on fire. *That's* what I wanted to do with my life, write like that.

"Oh, he'll see you," Herbert Gold said. "He sees everyone. He's a lovely man. A gossip. He loves to talk. But watch out for his wife. A terrible woman. A harridan. She guards him like a hawk. If she answers, you won't get in." The dark eyes flicked, on, off, on, off, one paratrooper boot flung over his knee, jiggling, tough stuff.

Gold was flying to Helsinki in the morning, he told me, interviewing Brigitte Bardot. For *Playboy*. He said the word softly. Was I impressed? The eyes skittered. And then to St Paul de Vence to talk to Marc Chagall. That was for *Playboy* too. I think he wanted me to ask him what Brigitte Bardot was doing in Helsinki but I didn't.

O.K., enough about Herbert Gold, he is not my main business here, I have introduced him here because he did this: He gave me the courage, when I got to New York, to pick up the phone and talk to a writer I otherwise wouldn't have dared to, a writer I have been reading for ten years and more with steadily growing admiration and awe. And, yes, love.

And I was lucky. I didn't get his wife.

"Come on Saturday. Four o'clock," said Isaac Bashevis Singer.

I was an hour early. I sat in Central Park. I brooded. I had doubts. What business did I have, I asked myself, interrupting Isaac Bashevis Singer? He is an old man, seventy-one or -two. What could I possibly say to him? Was I just a celebrity hunter, an autograph hound?

I almost didn't go. And then I summoned up exactly what it is that Isaac Bashevis Singer means to me. He has told me about my past. Singer was born in Poland, in Radzymin, a village, a *shtetl*, the son of a rabbi, and all his life he has written about that country, that way of life, the poverty, the pogroms and superstitions, the rites of marriage, the love of talmudic lore, furnishing his stories with the smells and sounds of that departed time to the finest detail, the crowing of cocks, the windows stuffed with rags, the creak of the peddlers' carts, the forests, the snow.

And I am Polish too, though born in Australia, but where Singer remembers and records, my parents chose to forget. They hinted at it, it was there in their eyes, the joys of those disappeared days, but whenever I asked for details, what it was like *exactly,* my parents' reply was always the same. "Ah, what would you understand, what would you know about such things?"

But I do know, and it is Isaac Bashevis Singer who has told

me. So how could I not go and see him, how could I not tell him this?

But now I was late. I had brooded too long. I hurried along the street where he lives, on the Upper West Side, searching for his address. I found it. Singer lives on the fourth floor. I went up in the lift. A young man opened the door. He ushered me in. Isaac Bashevis Singer sat in an armchair by a window, a pen in one hand, a sheaf of papers in the other.

He was writing.

Isaac Bashevis Singer is a small man, seemingly delicate, very pale. His voice is soft and high, with a slightly querulous tone. He rose from his seat, put down his papers, his pen. His eyes are a faded blue, but with something impish about them, something shrewd. He insisted I sit in his seat. He fetched for himself a straight-backed wooden chair. I looked around the apartment.

It was more French than New York, upper middle class Parisian, the rooms spacious and comfortably furnished, double doors, mirrors, a casual elegance. Isaac Bashevis Singer publishes regularly in *The New Yorker,* he has been in *Esquire* and *Playboy* too, magazines that pay handsomely for fiction. In *The New York Times* that morning I read that a play based on one of his stories was shortly to open on Broadway. His collection of stories, *A Crown of Feathers,* won the National Book Award. He is no longer the obscure Yiddish writer who came to New York in 1935, who for thirty years was known mostly only to the readers of the *Jewish Daily Forward,* where he published his stories and novels and memoirs, in Yiddish, that sadly diminishing tongue.

The young man who had let me in sat down on a settee. There was a girl beside him. Isaac Bashevis Singer introduced them. "They are helping me," he explained. "A film is to be made from one of my novels, *Enemies, A Love Story.* I am writing the screenplay myself. I am dictating it to these young people. I have never done such a thing before, but do you know, I am enjoying it, I find it easy."

That impishness for a moment was uppermost in his eyes, a merriness, a twinkle.

"But tell me," he said, moving a little closer on his chair, "who are you, why have you come?"

11

He had completely forgotten my phone call, my appointment for four o'clock.

I introduced myself. I told him about my parents, how indebted I was to him for furnishing me with a past. "Ah, a lot of young people say this to me," he said. He said this matter-of-factly, with no special pride, and I sensed then a European thing, that responsibility of learning that was so much a part of Old World life, that thing I had seen in my mother's eyes when I had told her I wanted to be a writer. In Europe, in *that* Europe, writers were important, they were respected, but not only that. It was the duty of a writer, an established writer, to pass on his knowledge, his learning, to the young, to counsel, to help, to advise. This is why, I felt, Isaac Bashevis Singer had consented to see me. He was upholding the European tradition.

We spoke for a while about writing, then about patronage, about government aid. I told him that I was on an Australian Government Literary Grant. "Do you know," he said, "I was offered by the Rockefellers, the Fords, to go to Switzerland, to go to Japan. It would be good there for my writing, they said, I would write better. They offered me a lot of money." He threw his hands in the air. "What do I want with Switzerland? What do I want with Japan? If you want to write, you will write. It is something inside you. You have it or you don't. That's all there is to it. If it's inside you, it will come out."

I commented then on what a fine magazine *The New Yorker* is, what a unique magazine, to publish a Yiddish writer who writes about goblins and spirits, evil spirits, *dybbuks,* superstitions, a vanished world. "*The New Yorker* is not important," he said. "If it didn't exist, no one would miss it. All the magazines. If all writing today disappeared, it wouldn't matter for a minute. We would live happily in the Nineteenth Century. With Tolstoy, with Chekhov, with Dostoyevsky. That's the great writers. Today is nothing. What's today? The avant-garde? I have read the avant-garde for fifty years. I read a few pages, I throw it away. It is nothing."

Isaac Bashevis Singer writes two sorts of stories. The first have to do with *shtetl* life. Singer is fascinated by the occult, the unexplained, the irrational. Evil spirits take people over. Strange

12

voices come out of their mouths. Rabbis are called. Rites are performed, prayers chanted, the *dybbuk* is exorcised. The world is unknowable, but the All Mighty prevails.

We can put these happenings down to the superstitions of a backward people, the ignorance of *shtetl* life, but Singer's attitude is ambivalent. In a story called *Why The Geese Shrieked,* which is in a memoir called *In My Father's Court,* he tells how a woman once brought two geese to his father, the rabbi, and said that they shrieked. Dead geese. Their heads had been cut off, they had been killed in the proper way, and still they shrieked. She picked up one goose and threw it down on the table. The goose shrieked. "Well, can anyone still doubt that there *is* a Creator?" the rabbi said. He began to wail and chant. But the rabbi's wife would have none of it. "It's the windpipes," she said. "You have neglected to take them out. That is why the geese continue to shriek." She tore them out. The geese were silent at last. And the rabbi, Isaac Bashevis Singer's father, what was his attitude now? "Your mother takes after your grandfather, the Rabbi of Bilgoray," he said to his son. "He is a great scholar, but a cold-blooded rationalist. People warned me before our betrothal . . ."

Isaac Bashevis Singer sits in both camps. He knows there is a rational explanation, but also that there is a Creator, capable of miracles, of *dybbuks* and sprites. But possibly his beliefs are not so important. What is important is that he remembers, he records.

But he writes other stories too, and these are even more interesting, stories where the Old World comes to New York. In the rubbing together of these two cultures, Singer has created a new literature.

"I must work now," Isaac Bashevis Singer said to me. "But please stay, if you would like. You will see how I write my screenplay." The blue eyes twinkled again. "No," I said, "I have taken too much of your time already." We shook hands. He showed me to the door. I walked back to sit in Central Park.

I thought about *Old Love,* which is one of the stories in a collection called *Passions.* An old man awakes at five o'clock in the morning. He can't sleep any more. He has been married several times, he has had mistresses, but they are all dead now, everyone is dead. He thinks fleetingly about them, frowns at the thought of marrying again, as people tell him he should. He is a rich man, exactly how rich he doesn't know himself. Two million? Three? He had left Poland when he was nineteen, a religious boy, strictly brought up, but in America he had forsaken that life. He went into business. He prospered. He grew rich.

That afternoon there is a knock on his door. It is a neighbour, a widow. She is lonely. She wants to talk. He reminds her of her late husband, she says. Something happens between them, very quickly. They hug and kiss. They talk of marriage. They are both very excited. He goes to her apartment. She makes lunch for them both. Then she says she wants to be alone for a while. He goes back to his apartment and falls asleep, and is woken by sounds of running outside. What is it? What has happened?

The widow has committed suicide, thrown herself from her balcony. She has left him a note. "Dear Harry, forgive me, I must go where my husband is. If it's not too much trouble, say Kaddish for me. I'll intercede for you where I'm going."

Harry is stunned, shocked. The widow has a daughter, run away from home, living in a tent in British Columbia. The story ends like this:

"An adventurous idea came into the old man's mind: to fly to British Columbia, find the young woman in the wilderness, comfort her, be a father to her, and perhaps try to meditate with her on why a man is born and why he must die."

Isaac Bashevis writes about my past, my parents' *shtetl* life, but don't see that as his limit. If you write about one place well, you write about everywhere.

An Open Letter To William Saroyan

Dear Mr Saroyan,

Are you well? Your photograph on the dust jacket of *Days of Life and Death and Escape to the Moon* (the English edition, Michael Joseph 1971) looks well. I am writing to this photograph, to the firm eye lines, to the nose in light, the chin in shade, to the deep moustache, to the crisp grey hat. The book is on the table before me, photograph side up. Hello, Mr Saroyan. How are you?

I am also writing to a copy of *The Daring Young Man on the Flying Trapeze* (the first edition, Random House 1934). I bought this book second-hand, it doesn't have a dust jacket, I am writing to the pale grey binding, the gold band across, the tall matt black spine. You are a young man in this book, full of beans. I clap your shoulders. Hello!

Also on my table (but I'm not writing to them) are The Pocket Oxford Dictionary, a jar of pencils, a ream apiece of quarto bond and quarto bank, white, an ashtray, a red Cricket cigarette lighter, two packs of Camels (one almost empty), a mottled grey marble paperweight in the shape of a little book. I am writing this on a pale green Hermes 3000.

I am thirty-nine years old, Mr Saroyan, an Australian writer of mostly short stories, sitting in my room in Melbourne, the room where I come daily to work.

Let me light a cigarette.

I'm writing to you, Mr Saroyan — well, I meant to write to you a long time ago. I meant to write to you when I was eighteen years old, and nineteen, and twenty, when I first discovered you, when I first discovered *The Daring Young Man on the Flying*

15

Trapeze, and *Inhale and Exhale,* and *Dear Baby,* and *My Name is Aram,* and those stories in *Esquire,* and those stories in *The Saturday Evening Post.*

Incredible days, incredible years! I was falling to pieces, Mr Saroyan, I didn't know what to do with myself, I didn't know what I was going to be (not that I especially wanted to be anything, but people kept asking), I was unhappy in college, about to quit, my mother was dying, I sat all day and half the night in the gloom of the Melbourne Public Library, under the great dome, surrounded by footsteps, whispers, the muffled cannon fire of books being closed with a bang.

Only I wasn't in the Public Library, I wasn't falling to pieces, my mother wasn't dying — I was in Fresno, I was in San Francisco, I was walking down the street in need of a haircut looking like several violinists out of work and worrying about the Assyrians, I was confiding to Greta Garbo, I was roaring through the countryside on a motorcycle I could never afford to own and didn't give a damn, one wild ride was enough for me, I was singing along with a scratched record, drinking free water, lighting the last cigarette in the world, freezing to death. I was leaping, sleeping, breathing, *being.*

Well, you know. I think I was already, then, flowing down that river of being a writer (my mother's sad eyes, my father's silent scorn), and what you did wasn't to make it less of a foolhardy venture, less of the greatest tragedy that can befall a rational man.

Yes, it's a crazy thing to do all right, I said, reading you in the Public Library, but so what? What isn't? The craziness seemed to me an asset. I needed craziness. Craziness was all I had.

I mean, look at William Saroyan, I said. Hello, Mr Saroyan, I said to you then. Greetings and good health! At eighteen, nineteen and twenty, though I was five years and more away from writing my first word, I was already flowing, feeling the current tugging at my feet. And you did this: You showed me some fancy dives.

I honestly meant to write to you then.

Years passed, elapsed. I travelled, moved to England, married, had children. Wrote. Published. Read. No, not you, Mr Saroyan. I don't know why, but not you.

16

From time to time, in my reading, I would come across a reference to you, to your books, to your work, and these references were always disparaging, sneery even. Critics. Reviewers. Sentimental, they said, about some writer or other and immediately compared him to you. Shmaltzy, they said, like Saroyan. Naive. Romantic. Dreamy, they said. Thin. And I felt pinpricks of outrage, remembering the Saroyan I read when I was eighteen, nineteen and twenty, the Assyrians, the haircut, the freezing to death in a room in San Francisco, but I hadn't read you for a long time, Mr Saroyan, I wasn't in any position (I told myself) to defend you, I had nullified my right to outrage.

Also I was busy. Serious business, this being a writer. Hard world. Toughness is the style. Deadlines. Bills to pay. Who had time for letter writing?

Well, something like that.

Words.

Excuses.

Nothing is ever completely true.

More years.

One Saturday morning I opened *The Guardian* and there was a piece about you. A full page. Lead feature. By a writer called Jack Trevor Storey. Mr Storey wrote *The Trouble With Harry*, which he claims to have sold to Alfred Hitchcock for a hundred pounds, outright, shortly after which he (Mr Storey) went bankrupt, and the last I heard of him, he was in Paris, driving around in a large American car, a soft-top Cadillac, I think it was, still bankrupt as bejeezus, still writing like crazy.

His books, if you don't know them, Mr Saroyan, are very funny. Nicely lunatic. I commend them to you.

That Saturday morning, in *The Guardian*, Jack Trevor Storey said you were as good as ever, and better than anyone thought. He said it was a disgrace that people didn't read you so much any more. He said you were terrific. He said you were a writer's writer, the ultimate compliment. He said he loved you. He wrote this on the occasion of the English publication of *Life and Death and Escape to the Moon*. I happened to see the book in a bookshop that morning. I bought it.

I read it that day. All of it. Couldn't stop reading it. Read it from cover to cover. What a marvellous book!

There you were, marching around Paris, charging up the avenues, down the boulevards, abstaining from coffee and tobacco (testy, proud), growing plants, brooding, musing, writing; and in Fresno, your old home town, walking, working, thinking, the same. The daring young man was older now, into middle age, and more, marking the deaths of famous contemporaries, seeing them fall, one by one (Garfield, Steinbeck, Gershwin, Sinclair Lewis), but you were still alive, still wonderfully alive, still daring. Still leaping, sleeping, breathing, *being*. Business as usual.

I was ashamed of myself, Mr Saroyan, as I read and read, for not having been with you all those years. Deeply ashamed. I read the book again, ashamed and marvelling. Then a third time.

I made immediate plans to write to you that instant.

Of course, I never did.

Now the story takes a leap of three or four years. I am in New York, talking to forty-one-year-old Burt Britton, employee at the Strand Book Store, also world's greatest reader (he claims, probably truthfully), sitting in his bookfilled apartment on West Eighty Sixth Street, Miles Davis softly on the stereo, scotch in our glasses. My wife is present, also Korby, Burt Britton's girl. It is about eight o'clock. We will go out to dinner soon.

I have known Burt Britton for only a few hours, but we are getting along famously. We are talking, of course, about books. Somewhere along the line the subject of the Nobel Prize comes up.

"Bellow's getting it," Burt Britton tells me. "He's the next American who is getting the Nobel Prize. It's practically official. Well, I think Bellow is terrific, a great writer, only you know who I think should get it first, and it's a disgrace they haven't given it to him after all these years — Tennessee Williams. Do you like Tennessee? And Bernard Malamud. Those two." I nod. Agreed. Fine writers both. "Of course," says Burt Britton, narrowing his eyes, "if there was any justice in the world, if things were done for the right reasons, forget the politics and all that crap, I'm talking about what the Nobel Prize is really about, there's only one American writer who should get it, the only one who fulfils all the requirements."

He leans forward, looks at me hard. "William Saroyan," he says.

18

"Ah!" I say. "You like William Saroyan?"

"*Like*?" he says, and just like that, goes into a scene from *The Time of your Life,* he and Korby, they know it by heart, the scene where the girl asks is the writer famous and the writer says yes and the girl asks is he published and he says of course not. Oh, they do it beautifully, he and she, speaking the words. Not a performance, not for me. For themselves, like a ritual, a thing they have together.

They finish. Burt Britton turns to me. "If you don't believe those people are in love by the time that scene is over," he says, "more in love than any two people in the history of the world, well . . ."

He puffs moodily on his cheroot. We are quiet for a moment, all four of us, in Burt Britton's book-filled apartment, playing that scene over in our heads.

I am happy.

"Do you read Saroyan?" Burt Britton asks me suddenly. "Of course," I tell him. "I love him. *Days of Life and Death and Escape to the Moon.*" "What else?" he says. "What other Saroyans have you got?" "Well," I tell him, "I can't remember all the titles . . ."

"If you don't know all the titles," Burt Britton says, "*you don't love Saroyan!*"

This is an accusation, a condemnation. Worse. He has found me out. Burt Britton extends his arms, indicating a vast length. "My Saroyan shelf," he says. "All of them. All his books. I've got every one. Every word he's ever written."

A silence falls. I am not a true Saroyan lover. I am in disgrace. "Well," I say, fighting to reinstate myself, "I've got a first edition of *The Daring Young Man on the Flying Trapeze.*"

"What!" cries Burt Britton, sitting bolt upright.

"Which contains," I tell him, rallying now, "The Preface to the First Edition, which is not, of course, in any other edition, also—"

Burt Britton is speechless, on the edge of his seat.

"Also," I continue, "there's a story which is not in any other edition, to the best of my knowledge, a story about going to a brothel and falling in love —"

Burt Britton continues speechless.

"Morris," says my wife, "why don't you send Burt the book?"

"Are you crazy?" I say. "Send it? Give it away" I lend books all over the place, give them away, never see them again, don't care, but I am suddenly possessive about my Saroyans. I am fiendishly possessive. I will kill to defend them.

"I'll make you a Xerox," I tell Burt Britton. "How's that? Anyhow, I need that book. I need it because I'm going to write to William Saroyan, I've been meaning to write to him for years, and —"

"You're going to write to him?" Burt Britton says, I can't tell whether pleased or amazed. "You're going to write to William Saroyan?"

"Of course," I say.

"I wrote to him," says Burt Britton. "Do you want to hear about it, about how I wrote to him?"

"Go on," I tell him.

"O.K.," he says, adjusting his cheroot.

"I wanted," Burt Britton says, "a drawing." Burt Britton collects drawings, self portraits by writers he likes. He has Mailer, Isaac Bashevis Singer, Janet Flanner, Robert Penn Warren, Bellow, Updike. He has an enormous number of them, which Random House will publish as a book.

"How could I not have Saroyan? I don't like just writing to someone out of the blue, though. I like to approach people personally if I can. But Saroyan? No way. He's never in town. I don't even know anyone who knows him.

"O.K. I thought about it, brooded. How do I get to William Saroyan? I got on to his daughter, Lucy. Took it slow. Months and months. Finally I felt ready, I told her about my collection, I said, Your father happens to be my favourite writer in the whole world. Don't ask me, Lucy said, I haven't spoken to him for years.

"Disaster! Wiped out! I brooded some more. I got on to Aram, his son. Well, just write to him, Aram said. He gave me his father's address. And back came this drawing, a Saroyan drawing, all wild and woolly, marvellous, beautiful! But wait a minute, he'd written under it, you know what he'd written? *Writers — how silly, how sad they are.*"

"I am writing to him," I say. "I am definitely writing —"

"But that's not all," Burt Britton says. "Underneath that, this: *Please return this drawing when it has fulfilled your purpose.*"

"I am writing," I say, "absolutely and definitely —"

20

"Well," says Burt Britton, "what to do? I wanted that drawing. I needed that drawing. O.K. I thought and thought. This is what I did. I drew eleven self portraits, put them into an envelope together with his drawing and said, How about trading eleven Burt Brittons for one William Saroyan? And back came — guess what? Not that William Saroyan drawing. No, sir. No way on earth he was going to let me have that. That one was his. I got — a brand new *different* William Saroyan self portrait!"

Burt Britton smiles, pleased. "Go figure that," he says.

"Crazy Armenian craziness!" I cry, leaping to my feet. "I am definitely writing, making full use of the Preface to the First Edition, plus anything else that comes to hand, and —"

And suddenly everyone is laughing, me and Korby and Burt and my wife, laughing like mad, and it's not just ordinary laughter either, it's the laughter of eighteen, nineteen and twenty, of motorcycles, of haircuts, of freezing to death with your last cigarette, of leaping, sleeping, breathing, *being*. All that.

And then we calm down and go out to dinner. We have a fine time.

Mr Saroyan, I sit in my room. I brood. I smoke. I write. Words.

I ask myself questions. Why haven't I written all these years? Why don't people read you so much any more?

Sentimental. Shmaltzy.

Words.

Napalm. Thalidomide. Pollution. Detente.

Words.

I open *The Daring Young Man on the Flying Trapeze*. I turn to the Preface to the First Edition. I read.

The most solid advice, though for a writer is this, I think: Try to learn to breathe deeply, really to taste food when you eat, and when you sleep, really to sleep. Try as much as possible to be wholly alive, with all your might, and when you laugh, laugh like hell, and when you get angry, get good and angry. Try to be alive. You will be dead soon enough.

Is it, Mr Saroyan, that you embarrass us, that you show us what we used to be? And you can blame us if we don't want to know?

Forgive us. Forgive me.

And please don't stop.

Yours sincerely,
Morris Lurie.

Destiny At Esquire

Gordon Lish, *Esquire's* fiction editor, won't tell we what he's paying Truman Capote. I think he's ashamed. Well, either that, or he's pretending to be ashamed, difficult to tell. Whatever, he's looking very vexed. I am sitting in his office, which is about the size of a waiting room at a tattooist's, such space as there is filled with Gordon's desk (which is tiny) and a chair for visitors (which is uncomfortable), plus two other chairs which Gordon whispers to me are extremely valuable antiques and they're in here because he hasn't got room for them in his miniscule apartment and also, another whisper, I wouldn't happen to know anyone prepared to pay the right kind of money for these little beauties? (which are, incidentally, totally unsittable, your absolute arsebreakers beside which no other chairs in the entire world come even close), but wait a minute, there's more, there's Gordon's hump-backed type-writer on its own little rickety stand, there are manuscripts all over the place, vital correspondence, memo pads, an ashtray the size of a car wheel, and then you get to the walls, which you can't see, because every square inch of them is covered with either a photograph of Barbara, Gordon's gorgeous blonde model wife, or a photograph of Atticus, Gordon's equally gorgeous six-year-old model son (he does TV commercials), or a photograph of Ken Kesey or James Dickey or Richard Selzer plus half a dozen other people, all those writers who think Gordon is tops, and in between the photographs are plaques and certificates acknowledging Gordon's contribution to the art of literature in these parlous times — wait a minute, I haven't finished, I haven't got to the windows yet . . . what windows? you can hardly see the windows, much less out of them, inasmuch as stacked up high in front of them (there are two) are literary quarterlies without number, hundreds at least, stacked and piled in such a way as to remove even one — to attempt to do so — would cause such an avalanche that the photograph of Ernest Hemingway, which is perched atop the right-hand window stack, would kiss this world good-bye.

Oh, I nearly forgot. Also in the room, right in the middle is a column, a post.

This is *Esquire*? This is the famous *Esquire*? This is what published Hemingway's *The Snows of Kilimanjaro*, that great, great story, and F Scott Fitzgerald's *The Crack Up* and Irwin Shaw and William Saroyan and John Cheever's *The World of Apples*, and well, every great writer you can think of, including seventeen (I think it is) Nobel Prize winners, and started off Tom Wolfe, and got Norman Mailer onto journalism, and Saul Bellow too (they got him to write about Kruschev), and . . .?

Hey, this is an historic place.

And I am harrassing Gordon Lish about the mundane matter of cash.

Meanwhile, Capote is in jail, drunk driving or some such thing, it was on the radio this morning, which gives you some idea of the standing in the community of the celebrated Tru, and Gordon is phoning and phoning, looking more worried by the minute, but Capote either can't talk to him or won't. I postulate that the legendary Tru is kneedeep in faggoty investigations right there in the jailhouse. Gordon looks terrified.

"Come on," I say. "How much are you paying?"

Esquire's standard fee for fiction is a measly six hundred and fifty dollars, and that involves a fight, but the price goes up if you're the right sort of person. Harold Brodkey got two thousand for a piece, a lovely piece, out of his novel-in-progress. Bellow got five for a slab of *Humbolt's Gift,* which Gordon didn't even want to publish but word came down from above: Do it! The most Gordon has ever paid, apart from to the wily Tru, is thirty. That was to Hemingway — to the Estate of, that is, in the person of the Widow Mary — for the Bimini section of *Islands in the Stream*. Gordon looks proud and perplexed at the same time when he tells me this.

"O.K.," I say, "but what about Tru?"

The Capote thing is a sore point with Gordon, or maybe he's

just pretending it is. *Esquire* publishes twelve, maybe fifteen pieces of fiction a year, and when you consider that *Esquire* can get practically anything in the world, any writer, you're talking about the most scrupulously handpicked stuff. Gordon is a legend in this town, loved and feared, a power, a myth, above all, respected. Left to his own devices, or so he says, Capote is the last living author with whom he desires to have truck, but once again the word came down from above: Do it! Capote, you understand, is a circulation builder, never mind his literary quality, so Gordon flew out to see him in California and came back with a story called *Mojave* which he published last year, and then it turned out that *Mojave* wasn't a story, it was a part of Tru's ten-years-in-the-making eagerly-awaited blockbuster novel *Answered Prayers*, so Gordon flew out again and came back with another hunk, and then a third one, and there's more to come. How much more? Is Capote going to parcel out the whole thing to *Esquire*, bit by bit? Gordon's lips are sealed.

"Gordon," I plead, "give me the word on Capote."

Answered Prayers, by the way, if you happen not to have read any of it, well . . . gossip. Dirty gossip. How the jet set fucks. It might have taken Tru ten years to write, but only five minutes of that to invent the names. Capote's characters move under the thinnest disguises ever concocted. And since Tru is a member of the jet set himself . . . what's he doing here? Shitting in his own nest? I mean, are these people happy to see their secrets blown?

"Fifty grand?" I ask Gordon. His eyes pop with alarm.

So now we move into the realm of conjecture. Why is Capote doing this? Stories abound, but the one that strikes a chord with me goes like this. Capote has been working on this novel for years and years. He shows bits of it to friends, thinking they're going to love it. Instead, they tell him it's awful, the worst thing he's ever done, maybe that anyone has ever done. Capote is crushed. Then he finds out he's got cancer. Dying. He rewrites his novel in the light of this discovery, makes it even more awful, really blows the whistle on the whole bunch of jet set fuckeroos, all the names, all the places, all the salacious details . . . I mean, what's he got to lose?

At the same time he spreads the word that what he's doing here in *Answered Prayers* is no less than what Proust did — Proust was dying too, you'll recall. Proust blew the whistle first.

Tru is simply following literary precedent.

Naah, come to think of it, I don't like that story either. Tru isn't dying. Truman Capotes don't die.

Anyhow, who cares, I've got other things on my mind. I am pressing the great Gordon.

"Forty?" I ask him. "Are you paying forty?" Gordon is in the middle of yet another attempt to talk to the jailed Tru, but he takes time off to show me the whites of his eyes.

So now you get the picture. Here is Gordon Lish, top arbiter of literary values, forced to publish . . . junk. He can no longer show his face in town. Where are his standards? Where is his famous editorial control, his unerring taste? Hell, *Answered Prayers* is not just filthy talk, it's . . . unreadable. What's he doing publishing junk like that?

"Give me a cigarette," Gordon says. "What ya smoking? Camels? Jesus. You know what those things are full of? Wait there, don't move, I'm going to bum me a cigarette."

Gordon rushes off, comes back a minute later with a cigarette so low in tar and nicotine and everything else a cigarette is supposed to have in it it's like smoking a piece of chalk. Americans are terrified of dying but they just can't stop smoking. Gordon chews gum at the same time as he smokes, both at a frantic rate.

Now he's phoning the jailhouse again, running a hand through his wispy hair, looking nervously at me. Nope. Capote won't or can't.

"Would you believe forty?" Gordon whispers to me.

"Per piece?" I ask. A tiny nod from Gordon. "Jesus."

"I know," he says. "I know."

I have never seen a human being looking so perplexed.

And then he says this to me, his voice so low I have to crane to hear:

"You know it's crap and I know it's crap but you know what's happening? You know that guy who was in here yesterday, top critic, I mean, *top* — I mean he's about the biggest there is. 'Gordon,' he says, 'that Capote you're running.' 'Yes?' I say to him, and Jesus, I can't even look him in the eye, that's how bad I feel about the whole business. 'Gordon,' he says, 'it's beautiful. It's the best thing I've ever read. It's absolutely . . . *great!*'"

Gordon looks at me and I look at him and neither of us knows what to say. We stare at each other in silence.

And then he swings back to his phone, to his cigarette, his gum, his hair. And I tiptoe out of that historic literary place, leaving Gordon to his own perplexity, to his destiny with the great Tru.

Vonnegut Lunch

I had arranged to be at Kurt Vonnegut's house at one o'clock. We would have lunch nearby, he had said. New York teetered on the edge of snow. First tentative flakes were actually falling. I had a long way to go, from the Upper West Side to East 48th Street, right over near the U N Building, that area of New York known as Turtle Bay. I had trouble getting a cab. The first thing I said to Kurt Vonnegut, when he came downstairs, was how sorry I was to be late. Kurt Vonnegut looked at his watch. "Seven minutes," he said. Then he went upstairs again.

So it goes.

"So it goes" is a phrase Kurt Vonnegut employed in *Slaughterhouse-Five*, the novel that brought him world fame. He used it to terminate many of the short paragraphs of which the book is composed. It gave the effect of a kind of shrug, a gesture of helplessness, a near-mute acceptance of how things are, or were.

Kurt Vonnegut was a prisoner of war in the Second World War. He was in a slaughterhouse in Dresden when the city was firebombed. The bombs sounded to him like giant footsteps above. "The giants walked and walked," he wrote. When he emerged from the slaughterhouse, the once beautiful city of Dresden no longer existed. It took him twenty years to find a way to talk about this in his fiction. So it goes.

Kurt Vonnegut lives with Jill Krementz, a photographer who specialises in photographing writers. The smiling Kurt Vonnegut in a three-piece chalk-striped suit standing in a park on the dust jacket of the American edition of *Slapstick*, his latest novel, is her work. Kurt Vonnegut looks there, as he does in real life, as though he would have had no trouble playing the part of a waiter in a Lubitch comedy in the 40s. He looks kind-hearted and wise and slightly wacky.

Jill Krementz was talking to an assistant when I arrived, a girl who looked like an *au-pair*. Jill was flying to Boston in the morning and needed to have certain photographs ready. She is a small, slim, dark-haired attractive young woman who moves with New York intensity. It is in her eyes, too, when she looks at you, but there, you feel, it masks a certain vulnerability.

I looked at the framed photographs in the hall. Kurt Vonnegut had come downstairs and gone up again. The photographs are by Jill Krementz and by people she admires. I played with Pumpkin, the Vonnegut dog, one of those tiny long-haired terriers who bark like crazy but are a pushover in a wrestle. It was nice being in a house, a real house, after all those New York apartments. The ground floor of the Vonnegut townhouse is two large rooms opened up and flowing into a kitchen at the end which overlooks a small garden. It is like a house in London, in Kensington, say, or Holland Park. I remembered reading somewhere that after *Slaughterhouse-Five* Kurt Vonnegut had signed a contract for his next three books, sight unseen, which guaranteed him a million dollars. Jill Krementz finished giving instructions to her assistant. She turned to me. There was that intensity, there was that vulnerability in her eyes. "Am I going to need a photograph of you?" she asked me.

Hi ho.

"Hi ho" is the phrase Kurt Vonnegut uses in *Slapstick* as he used "So it goes" in *Slaughterhouse-Five*. He apologizes for it, though. "It is a kind of senile hiccup," he has the elderly narrator of the book say. "I have lived too long. I swear: If I live to complete this autobiography, I will go through it again, and cross out all the 'Hi ho's.' " But he doesn't. There are "Hi ho's" all over the place. Kurt Vonnegut is fifty-five years old, which is not, to my way of thinking, an elderly narrator. I hadn't read *Slapstick* when we had our lunch together. Which is just as well, because when I did I didn't like it much.

Hi ho.

Kurt Vonnegut came downstairs again. He put on a winter-lined oatmeal-coloured poplin coat. He asked Jill Krementz if she would like to join us. "Where are you going?" she asked. She said to go ahead, she would join us there. Kurt Vonnegut and I stepped outside. We walked together down the street, in the direction of the river. Kurt Vonnegut is tall, six feet something. The snow had stopped. It was windy and cold. Both of us walked with our hands in our pockets. Very soon, I thought, I will know the answer to a question that has been vexing me for a week.

We went around the corner and down some steps into one of those restaurants where you are hardly aware that your coat is being removed, a chair being slid under you, a waiter whispering in your ear that the asparagus is fresh today. We ordered and got at once two glasses of red wine. Kurt Vonnegut pulled a crumpled pack of Pall Malls from the outside breast pocket of his jacket. I lit one for him, lit myself a Camel. We sipped our wine. Now, I thought. Now he'll tell me.

The morning after Kurt Vonnegut had said "Let's have lunch," and given me his phone number and told me to call, I had phoned Burt Britton. "Why has Kurt Vonnegut asked me to lunch?" I asked him. Burt Britton knows everything to do with the New York literary world. In fact, it was at the party to launch Burt Britton's book of over seven-hundred self-portraits by literary folk that I had met Kurt Vonnegut and been invited to lunch, and how that happened was like this: Someone pointed out Kurt Vonnegut to me, I went over, told him I was from Australia, a fan, shook his hand, and was about to walk away when he said "Let's have lunch."

"Why is he doing this?" I asked Burt Britton. "Because he *wants* to have lunch with you!" Burt Britton shouted in my ear, as though I didn't understand anything. "Kurt is like that," he said. "He's a beautiful person. Do it, Morris, do it. Call him. Have lunch. And listen, phone me straight after, I want to *hear!*"

We sipped our wine, Kurt Vonnegut and I. He didn't seem to want to say anything. He seemed exceedingly polite. I said that for the past three weeks I had been walking around New York with the distinct feeling that I was leaking money. He smiled. A Vonnegut smile takes place under his drooping moustache, with no show of teeth. What you see is a crinkling around the kind, brown eyes, a kind of dimpling in the cheeks. Before *Slaughter-*

31

house-Five made him world-famous, Kurt Vonnegut had enjoyed a growing underground or specialist reputation. Graham Greene had called him "one of the best living American writers". Science-fiction is an area of literature I tend to avoid, but I read *The Sirens of Titan,* which is science-fiction, spellbound, in a sitting. It was, and is, a lovely book.

I told Kurt Vonnegut how guilty I felt being in New York without my children; I could cater to my every whim without any trouble, but how difficult I found it to buy them the right gifts. Kurt Vonnegut has six children. He recommended the gift shop in the U N Building. "They've got beautiful things there from countries all over the world," he said. I said I'd check it out. He told me some of the things they had there. Small talk. I felt myself becoming infected with his politeness, by the restaurant's expensive hush. We smoked. We sipped our wine. Is this really the author of *The Sirens of Titan,* that wildly crazy fantastic book? I thought. Then Jill Krementz joined us, looking intense and vulnerable.

The waiter handed us double-foolscap-size leather-bound menus. Kurt Vonnegut and Jill Krementz opened theirs at once. I told Kurt Vonnegut that the most elegant orderer of food I had ever met was a British World War One Air Ace who never looked at the menu, absolutely ignored it, simply told the waiter what he felt like eating, and always got it. I thought the story would appeal to Kurt Vonnegut, to his sense of wackiness, but maybe I told it badly. His kind brown eyes looked puzzled. "What war?" he said. He studied his menu for a long time before ordering Eggs Benedict. Jill Krementz and I ordered Dover Sole. Spinach to go with it. Hi ho.

I brought up the subject of editing in America. I told Kurt Vonnegut about a New York writer I knew who had allowed a magazine editor to squeeze a hundred pages of a novel down to a six-page short story. "No English editor would dare do such a thing," I said. Kurt Vonnegut told me how he had once taught creative writing at a university somewhere, and what happened was, everyone in the class wrote a story and then each story was criticised by every member of the class and then all the stories were rewritten and rewritten until finally they pleased everyone. "That's terrible," I said. "Only one student committed suicide," Kurt Vonnegut said. "One out of forty. That's not a bad average. I used to think of giving them *Moby Dick*," he said, "and letting them criticise it and rewrite it until what we got was a perfectly acceptible *Moby Dick*. And then we could publish it and everyone would be happy." Another Vonnegut smile, under the drooping moustache.

We talked about this particular writer, whose work had been so edited. Kurt Vonnegut knew him too. "He's been writing his novel for over ten years," I said. "He doesn't teach, he doesn't do anything else. How do writers like that stay alive?" "His publisher has given him a hundred thousand," Kurt Vonnegut said. "Ten here, ten there. Kept him going. Everyone in New York gets money like that. You don't have to write any books. All you need is an idea. Half the time you don't even need that. I hate to think how much money has been laid out for books that will never be written. It's the American way." He said this seriously, or anyway matter-of-factly. I said that I couldn't work like that, being paid in advance. I needed the fear of poverty. I liked the wolf at the door. This is not strictly true, if it's true at all, but I felt myself being forced to take a contrary position. It was Kurt Vonnegut's soft-spoken politeness, it was the restaurant's expensive hush. "That's how he gets his kicks," Kurt Vonnegut said to Jill Krementz, as though he'd successfully pigeonholed me at last.

But this was still small talk, where was the real business of our lunch? I brought up the subject of Australia. Kurt Vonnegut had been invited to attend Writer's Week, a thing which the South Australian Government holds every two years, and he had accepted, but at the last minute he hadn't shown up. This was six months ago. I asked Kurt Vonnegut what had happened. He said that there had been family trouble, it was a bad time, his daughter had broken off her engagement, he had had to be there. "She's suicidal," Kurt Vonnegut said.

You can take a remark like that in all sorts of ways, but not from Kurt Vonnegut. His mother committed suicide. His son, Mark, is schizophrenic; Mark has written a book about his troubles. I looked at Kurt Vonnegut's crinkled kind brown eyes and I began to understand the excessive politeness, and later, when I read *Slapstick*, I felt it again, that soft-spoken politeness that has to be there because otherwise, you feel, anything could happen.

But there were other things too, other reasons he hadn't come to Australia. "It's not your Government that pays the fare," Kurt

Vonnegut said. "It's Fullbright money. And you know what that is. German reparations. Blood money. I don't want to take that." In *Slaughterhouse-Five* Kurt Vonnegut lists himself as a fourth-generation German-American. In Dresden he was being bombed by his own kin. So it goes.

"And they make you work for that money," Kurt Vonnegut went on. "I mean, *hard*." I lit another Pall Mall for him. I couldn't quite understand what he was saying. "Australia is so far," he said. "How long does it take to get out there? What's the first-class fare?" He asked me what Australia was like. I said that on the surface it could disappoint him, it was, or seemed to be, a sort of small-town America in the 50s, but it wasn't really, not if you were *quiet*, not if you *looked*. I said that it was a good place and that he should come out. He smiled. He seemed to like this.

We had coffee, Jill Krementz asked me about work in England, how much photographers were paid, things like that, and that was lunch. My coat appeared around me as magically as it had been whisked away. Outside, in the windy street, I put out my hand to say good-bye. "No, walk me back," Kurt Vonnegut said.

I asked him about Turtle Bay. He told me that Katherine Hepburn had a house down the end, an editor of *The New York Times* lived opposite, he pointed out the houses of other famous folk. I said, "Didn't E B White use to live here?" and he said yes, but he'd left a long time ago, in the 50s, he'd moved out to Maine. "He got scared," Kurt Vonnegut said. "He couldn't stand New York any more. In the 50s! He should see it now."

Back in the house, Kurt Vonnegut asked me to write down my address in Australia. I did. He asked me what I'd written, was any of it available. We stood in the kitchen. "Well, this boy has to get back to work," he said, shook my hand, and up the stairs he went, two at a time, a long-legged lope.

I had to go to *The New Yorker*, see an editor there. Jill Krementz was going that way. We walked together. When we said good-bye I was as puzzled as ever. What was that lunch really all about? I told the *New Yorker* editor about it. I told him that Kurt Vonnegut had made me write down my address in Australia. The editor's eyes flashed.

"Kurt Vonnegut is an alcoholic!" he burst out. "You know what he's going to do, don't you? He's going to *land* on you in

Australia! He's going to stay for *six months*! He's going to *drink you dry*!"

I thought this was an interesting theory, and, a couple of weeks later, back in Australia, I wrote to Kurt Vonnegut to ask him if this was his plan. I said that I didn't mind, in fact I would be flattered, but warned him that my liquor supply would never see six months. It was a nice letter, and I didn't expect a reply, and sure enough, I didn't get one. So it goes. Hi ho.

Afternoon in Ossining

Travelling to see John Cheever, on the 12:50 from Grand Central, nervous as hell, I looked at the cliffs of the Hudson River, the trees and mists, December, cold, and thought: This is the last view of America some people ever have. How many handcuffed murderers, I thought, more nervous by the minute, have looked out of this train, tried to print on their brains these final images of their land? John Cheever lives at Ossining, an hour out of New York, but the town is not, as it should be, famous for that, but for a harsher reality. For Ossining is the grey walls of Sing Sing, the dream gone sour, the end of the line.

We were coming into a station. I stood up. A woman said to me, "Oh, this isn't Ossining yet. Don't worry, I'll tell you." Smiling. American politeness. But before the next stop I stood up again. I was *that* nervous.

Why nervous? Because John Cheever is, for me, simply the best. But more than that. My business, my main business, is the writing of short stories, but periodically this happens: my bones grow soft, my breath falls short, I can't seem to focus my eyes, and when I speak, or try to speak, there is no recognisable voice. I feel intimidated and insubstantial, fraudulent, crushed. I can argue it out any way I like, adopt a hundred different stances, a thousand, but the central position remains unalterable: The writing of short stories is no fit job for a grown man. A month passes, two, on one dreadful occasion it took the entire length of a whole dreadful year, but in each case I am brought back, joyfully, redeemed, always in the same way. I read *The Death of Justina,*

37

The World of Apples, The Swimmer, The Wapshot Chronicle, Bullet Park. I read John Cheever.

Ossining!

"How will I recognise you?" John Cheever had asked.

"Oh I will be wearing," I told him, "a very dirty sheepskin-lined canvas Swedish Army officer's coat. It's incredibly dirty. It must be the dirtiest Swedish Army officer's coat in the world. I think it belonged to a deserter."

On the telephone, already nervous.

But I recognized him at once. Shetland sweater, corduroy jeans, yachting sneakers, tweed jacket, A writer's clothes. And the eyes, The quick smile. Sixty-four or -five years old, lined face, grey hair, but still with that boyish something — some people keep it forever, Cheever certainly will — a rascal, a scamp. But a courteous rascal, courtly, well brought up.

I came up the steps from the platform. Shook hands. In his other hand he held a cigarette. The ashtray in his small red car overflowed with butts. Vantage. The filter with the funny hole in the middle. "This isn't an interview, is it?" Cheever asked. Ill at ease. Yachting sneakers stomping on the pedals. "No," I said. "Nothing like that. I'm a fan." "Oh," he said, lighting another cigarette.

I asked him about his new novel, when it was due out. This was *Falconer. Playboy* had run a part of it some months before. The opening section. A tantalizing taste. "March," he said. "I've given it to Saul Bellow. Saul's a good friend. Well, the Nobel . . ." All writers are anxious about books to come out, but Cheever seemed to me exceedingly so. I said that I hadn't thought much of Bellow's latest, *Humbolt's Gift.* All that endless ranting and raving. "Well," I said, "there was one good bit, about fifty or sixty pages, and that's where Bellow stopped all the ranting and told a story. The bit about the gangster in Chicago. That was terrific," I said. "Story telling is out of fashion," I said. "Everyone is into Borges and Barthelme, all that fragmented stuff, games, but I think stories are the most important things we have. I can't be bothered with all that fragmented stuff," I said. "I like *The Country Husband.*" "I wrote that straight out," Cheever said. "I was on a train. Snowbound for two days. Wonderful! I wrote and wrote. Hemingway liked that story. So did Nabokov."

We were in the centre of Ossining. "Have you eaten," he asked me, "have you had lunch?"

We sat at a table in the back of a pub. A waitress handed me a menu. Cheever shook his head. He lit another cigarette. "What are you drinking?" he asked me. I said a glass of red wine would be fine. Cheever seemed disappointed. "Is that all?" he said. "Sure," I said. "I'm not really a big drinker. Well, not at this time of day." He seemed even more disappointed. The waitress took my order. "Just a Coke for me," Cheever said. He looked, well, not exactly sad, but not right either. I had been warned about this. "Cheever's on the wagon," a friend had told me, "He's in A.A. It got very bad. I don't know what kind of time you'll have up there with him. When he was drinking he was marvellous."

There is a story of Cheever's, a magnificent story, about a man whose wife simulates fornication nightly in an Off-Broadway play. It is called *The Fourth Alarm* and it begins like this: "I sit in the sun drinking gin. It is ten in the morning. Sunday. Mrs. Uxbridge is off somewhere with the children. Mrs. Uxbridge is the housekeeper. She does the cooking and takes care of Peter and Louise." That's the whole first paragraph, the way it appears in the collection called *The World of Apples,* but when the story first came out, in *Esquire,* the paragraph continued: "You might think ten in the morning a little early for a full glass of gin, but I regard my liquor with more praise than foreboding. I have had my liver measured and my blood tested. My health is perfect and I love my gin. It has gotten me calmly through forced landings, gruesome marital difficulties and capsized sailboats, and when this glass is empty I will pour another."

"But why did you take those lines out in the book?" I asked. "I mean, they're terrific." "Oh really?" Cheever said. "They weren't there? I don't recall . . ."

Oops, wrong subject. I fled to something else. I said how much I loved *The Death of Justina.* "Yes, that's a wonderful story," Cheever said. "It starts 'So help me God it gets more and more preposterous, it corresponds less and less to what I remember and what I expect as if the force of life were centrifugal' " — he reeled it off, knew it perfectly — "and it ends up with the Twenty-Third Psalm! I love reading that story out. The trouble is, people laugh too much. I mean, it *is* funny, but last week, when I read it, there was one woman who just wouldn't stop. A wonderful story. I'm going to read it again next week." He told me where. A college.

I asked him what it had been like teaching at Sing Sing. Cheever taught fiction there for a year. "I had three murderers, two rapists and an arsonist," he said. "I had a hell of a job getting in. No one had ever done that kind of thing before. I enjoyed it. Some of those people had never ever read a book. One of them, the arsonist, is having his first book published next year. A novel. I used to feel, every time I went in there, God, I'll never get out. But I enjoyed it."

Falconer is set in a prison clearly modelled on Sing Sing. The hero or central character is a forty-eight-year-old drug-addicted Professor of English in for fraticide whose wife says, when he asks her how the house is, "Well, it's nice to have a dry toilet seat." But it is not a bitter book — nothing that Cheever has written is bitter — and its last words are "Rejoice, he thought. Rejoice."

The Cheevers live in an eighteenth-century house with broad stone steps and a terrace and a view of distant neighbours and trees. Sing Sing is not visible, in another world. We stopped first at the mailbox, which is on the highway, before you turn in to his road. The mail that day was a huge box from *The New York Times*. I sat with it on my lap as we drove up to the house. The moment I got out of the car the Cheever dogs were all over me, golden retrievers, three of them — "That one's English," Cheever told me proudly — lovely dogs, friendly and frisky, but I couldn't help thinking of Cheever's story called *Metamorphoses* where a man breeds a Finnish wolf bitch to a German shepherd dog ("the American Kennel Club refused to list the breed") and he comes home one night and gets torn to pieces, but I didn't, of course, mention this, as I patted the dogs.

Cheever's wife, Mary, was in the kitchen, cooking. Tomorrow was Thanksgiving. Mary has a high Bostonian voice and the facial structure of a beauty. Before I had my coat off, Cheever asked me what I'd like to drink. I had learnt my lesson with the red wine — that sad look — and this time said whiskey. The box from *The New York Times* was two huge bottles of French champagne — payment for a piece Cheever had written about Thanksgiving turkeys he had known. He looked at the bottles sadly, and then got himself another Coke.

Logs burned in the wide grate. The dogs frisked, wanted to go out, wanted to be let in. I sipped my whiskey. "This isn't an interview?" he asked me again. I had just read an interview with Cheever. This was in *The Paris Review*. "They did that years ago," Cheever said. "Never used it. They must have thought I was dead." He smiled ruefully. "Anyhow, as a writer. They sent up this young girl. She was beautiful. When we played back the tape all you could hear was me saying, 'Let's get drunk and talk about Venice, let's get drunk and talk about Venice.' Someone else came up too. A very unhappy woman. We embraced with ardour in the pantry." The rascal, the scamp, shone in his eyes. "You sure you don't want another drink, let me freshen that up . . ."

Then Mary said could he go down to the liquor store, they needed some whiskey, vermouth and gin. "I'll go with you," I said, putting down my whiskey. "Oh, and a small ham," Mary said. "How small?" Cheever asked. "You know, just a small one," Mary said.

Then this happened:

Going out to the car, I saw that John Cheever's jacket was twisted around the collar and I reached over and straightened it. That was it. That was all. Cheever didn't say anything and neither did I, but my act, my impulsive act, affected me profoundly. It seemed to me, suddenly, that I had been impertinent, I was a stranger, I had taken an uncalled for liberty. I had drawn attention to Cheever's age. Or was I reading too much into what was, after all, the most uncluttered of gestures? I didn't know then and I don't know now, all I know is that it affected me profoundly.

We bought the liquor and the ham — Cheever said how much he liked supermarkets, what wonderful places they were, and liquor stores too, the labels, like fireworks — and then we drove back to the house.

"I have never been a money player," Cheever said. "I have been poor most of my life." He told me how he had continued to publish in *The New Yorker* when he could have got a lot more publishing in other magazines. "No, I've never been a money

41

player," he said again, and then he told me that someone had offered a lot of money for the film rights to *Falconer*. "A hundred thousand dollars," he said, but the figure didn't seem to cheer him. He got up, sat down, got up again. The dogs. The fire. His cigarettes. His fingers were restless on his empty glass. He was worried about *Falconer*. "I don't know what Saul will do, if he'll review it," he said. "I haven't seen him since the Nobel . . ."

The Nobel Prize seemed to hang heavy on him. Did he want it, grieve for it, that fake political plum? Surely not.

I thought of *The World of Apples,* that glorious story, which begins like this: "Asa Bascomb, the old laureate, wandered around his work house or study — he had never been able to settle on a name for a house where one wrote poetry — swatting hornets with a copy of *La Stampa* and wondering why he had never been given the Nobel Prize. He had received nearly every other sign of renown. In a trunk in the corner there were medals, citations, wreaths, sheaves, ribbons and badges. The stove that heated his study had been given to him by the Oslo P.E.N. Club, his desk was a gift from the Kiev Writer's Union, and the study itself had been built by an international association of his admirers. The Presidents of both Italy and the United States had wired their congratulations on the day he was presented with the key to the place. Why no Nobel Prize? Swat, swat."

Was this a portrait of Cheever, a self portrait? Surely not.

"I was talking to Burt Britton at the Strand Book Store," I said, "and he's a great admirer of Bellow, but do you know who he said should have got the Nobel Prize?"

"Who?" Cheever's face lit up.

"William Saroyan."

"Oh."

My God, he did want it. I felt saddened and perplexed, then other thoughts came galloping in. *I am not a money player.* This in a society where success is measured first and foremost in money. *I have been poor most of my life.* John Cheever has written four novels and more than a hundred and fifty stories, stories so fine, it seems to me, that a dozen at least will be read as long as the language exists, but Cheever himself will never be famous, not show-biz famous, he is too special for that, too humane. So why the Nobel Prize? Cheever knows what he is doing, he has

42

always known, but there must be moments, all writers have them, when a sign is needed, an outside sign, some vindication for the course of one's life.

Nothing would delight me more than Cheever getting it, but I don't think he will. There isn't that kind of rightness in the world.

And Asa Bacomb didn't get it either. What he did was to step naked into a waterfall, as he had seen his father once do. In the freezing water he bellowed, as his father had done too. The story ends ". . . and in the morning he began a long poem on the inalienable dignity of light and air that, while it would not get him the Nobel Prize, would grace the last months of his life."

In the pub Cheever had told me that he had just come back from Bulgaria. "What's in Bulgaria?" I had asked. "Waterfalls!" Cheever had said, eyes instantly alive. "The most wonderful waterfalls!"

Oh, one last thing. Driving me back to the station, almost there, John Cheever suddenly said, "You're right about *Humbolt's Gift*. That story about the gangster *is* the best part of the book. Yes."

Portrait of the Reader with a Million and a Half Books

1. Courting

It is four o'clock in the morning in New York City and Norman Mailer won't go home. Refuses. Sits. Everyone else has gone home. Well, not quite everyone. The maitre d' at the Village Vanguard, which is where Norman Mailer is sitting, is still here. He can't go until Mailer does. He has to close up. He wants to close up. The licensing laws of New York·State forbid the sale of alcohol after four o'clock in the morning, for a start. More than that, he is tired. He wants to go to bed. He has to get up early and audition for a part in a movie. Maitre d' at the Village Vanguard is only a part-time thing. In real life he's an out-of-work actor. Norman Mailer, however, continues to sit. The maitre d' sits with him, pleading. "Please go home, Norman," he says. "It's late. It's four o'clock in the morning, for God's sake." Norman Mailer is not swayed. He begins to hit the maitre d', pummel him, that is, light zinging upperarm shots betraying Mailer's Brooklyn origins, semi-friendly nudging punches, schoolboy stuff. "O.K.," says Mailer, "what do you want from me?" Norman Mailer is, of course, rich, famous and esteemed, but he believes, New York fashion, that everyone is on the hustle, on the make, wants something from him. Punch, punch. "Norman, I want to go home," says the maitre d'. "I want to close up. I want to go to *bed*." Punch, punch. "C'mon," says Mailer. "What do you want?" The maitre d' offers Mailer one last (illegal) drink for the road on the condition that he will then depart. No deal. Mailer won't go. Punch, punch. "C'mon. What?" This goes on for some time. Then the maitre d' does something strange, something which he afterwards won't be able properly to explain. He picks up a piece of paper which is lying on the table, a menu, the back of a bill, something like that, hands Mailer a pen, says, "I want you to draw yourself, Norman. I want a self-portrait. That's what I want from you." "Huh?" says Mailer, but the idea appeals to him, he draws, he signs, he goes home. So begins . . .

Now the story takes a skip of some years and I am in New York, in the tiny cluttered office of Gordon Lish, fiction editor of *Esquire* magazine. Gordon is a terrific guy but is not the hero of this piece. His role is to pass on to me a message. "Hey," he says, "Burt Britton wants to see ya. Wants ya to do a drawing of yourself. He's at the Strand. You know the Strand?"

Do I know the Strand? The Strand Book Store, on Lower Broadway at Twelfth Street, in the heart of New York's second-hand-book area, is the Garden of Eden. It is a treasure house. It is a trap. I am terrified of the Strand Book Store. In just two visits to the Strand Book Store I have kissed my burial money good-bye twice over and made purchase of more books than I will have time to read in eighteen years. The Strand Book Store boasts a stock of a million and a half books (I think it actually has more) which can be subdivided as follows: remaindered books (books in New York seem to be remaindered eleven minutes after they're published), review copies (often available before publication, and on sale at half price), and legitimate second-hand books. And I have bought, let me make plain, unstintingly in all categories.

But what's this drawing? Who is Burt Britton? Who cares? My ego zooms. I am known! Back at the Chelsea Hotel, where I am staying, I peer at my visage in the black-speckled mirror (which could be the very mirror into which Dylan Thomas similarly peered), and on Chelsea Hotel notepaper rapidly sketch what is before me, a likeness that could be slipped into Picasso's folio (Early Cubist Period) without anyone ever being the wiser. This I put carefully into a small paper carry bag and off to the Strand I go.

At the sales counter at the Strand Book Store I inquire of a tall burly man wearing half-moon spectacles on the tip of his nose the whereabouts of one Burt Britton. "Downstairs," he growls, not looking at me. I am about to turn when he snaps, "No bags!"

"Oh, it's just a drawing," I tell him. "I have to—" Now he looks at me, really looks. What could be a sneer plays about his lips. "Congratulations!" he booms, towering over me. "You're in the book!"

What?

I make my way downstairs, trying not to look at any books. The Strand Book Store is a labyrinth. Downstairs is even worse. "Where's Burt Britton?" I ask a girl. She points. Right at the back. EMPLOYEES ONLY says a sign. A roped-off area. More books. "Are you Burt Britton?" I ask a young man who is carrying books from one pile to another. He shakes his head, points behind a mountain of books, a veritable Everest of literature. "Burt!" he calls. "Someone here to see ya!" "Out in a minute!" comes a voice. I wait. Minutes come and go. I am getting tired. I am wearing Earth Shoes, which have no heel. My tendons are in agony, my feet on fire. More minutes come and go. My eyes start to close. Suddenly a figure appears, darts out from behind the mountain, roaring. "Don't lean on the books!"

Burt Britton (the hero of this piece) looks more like a hard-line negotiator for a tough union than a person connected with books. Tall. Burly shoulders. Dark darting eyes that look as though they can sniff out a situation in a second. A toughie. No crap brooked. Wearing tight jeans, a hide vest over a rolled-up-sleeves shirt, a red kerchief around the throat. Between the teeth, a foul-smelling cheroot. Got him? No, you haven't, because I haven't mentioned his hair, which is a parted-in-the-middle rapidly-greying black business waterfalling into a semi-unruly beard. This, together with his gold-framed spectacles, gives him a definite Rasputin ambience, a New York Bolshevik, sort of. Forty-one or -two years old. Moves with speed. ·

I introduce myself. He seems delighted. We shake hands. Burt's voice is a corner-of-the-mouth whisper that goes into a shout without preamble or warning, and when he talks you don't interrupt. Burt is a river making its own way to the sea. He whips out from somewhere a copy of my first novel, written and published ten years ago, the sales of which came perilously close to nudging double figures, a true underground classic and no mistake. And not only does he have it, but he has it wrapped in tough plastic — the toughest! bulletproof! — as though he too knows its true

47

worth. I am, naturally, astounded, delighted, in a spin. Curious thing, this fame. "Listen, sign your name in that," Burt says, "I've gotta answer the phone."

And the drawing, the self-portrait? Burt Britton comes back. This time he is holding a stack of drawings, Xerox copies, and while I flick through them (John Updike, Bernard Malamud, Isaac Bashevis Singer) he tells me that this is his hobby, his thing, he collects self-portraits by writers he likes, also illustrators, poets (Janet Flanner, Saul Bellow, Calvin Trillin, Joyce Carol Oates), it all started with Norman Mailer, he tells me, he tells me the whole thing (John Hollander, Penelope Gilliatt, James Salter, Maurice Sendak), and another thing, see, Random House have given him an advance, they want to publish his collection, so would I mind signing this release, saying it's O.K. for my drawing to be in the book. I sign with speed. "Jesus, that phone!" says Burt, whipping behind his books again.

While he's gone, I continue through the Xerox pile. Hey, everyone's here, what a collection. Robert Penn Warren, Susan Sontag. I note that some writers can draw very nicely (Isaac Bashevis Singer, John Updike, Terry Southern), some are lousy (Janet Flanner, for some reason, has drawn a Christmas tree; Mavis Gallant's self-portrait is a crammed page of sketches and words, an account of a typical day in her life). Naturally, I am thrilled to pieces to be in this august company, lousy drawings notwithstanding. "Hey, when's the book coming out?" I ask Burt Britton, when next he appears. "Well," he says, "I'm not so sure."

There are difficulties. For a start, he hasn't got *all* the writers he wants, he hasn't got Nabokov, hasn't got Borges, hasn't got Gabriel Garcia Marquez. Burt Britton doesn't like approaching writers cold, springing out of nowhere his request for a drawing. He regards writers as special people, possessed of a rare privilege, and acts accordingly. Writers, to Burt Britton, are heroes. He likes to get to know them, approach them personally. "Nabokov is a problem," he admits, "but you never know. He could drop in one day."

Another difficulty is that the fame of this book has spread, all sorts of people want to get into it, keep dropping hints, worse, actually come around with self-portraits, and well, they're ruining the whole idea of the book, which has to have only people Burt Britton *likes*. "Throw the drawings out," I counsel him sagely.

48

"Yeah," he says, "and what happens when the book comes out and they see they're not in it? I have to live in this town, Morris." He puffs on his foul cheroot, looks edgy, those dark darting eyes, visualizing savage New York ostracism, back stabbing, feuds.

But there is another difficulty, the main difficulty, unspoken by Burt Britton, but rapidly apparent to this shrewd observer. This collection is Burt Britton's *thing*, his uniqueness, he sort of hates to go public with it, hates the idea of letting it go. New York is a city of carefully guarded uniquenesses. Well, but he's signed with Random House, accepted the advance . . .

"Hey, did you come across the Tomi Ungerer yet?" Burt Britton asks. "Before you look at it, let me explain. He did the drawing, right? And I looked at it, and then I looked at him, and then I said, 'Tomi, you heard what I said, didn't you? A self-portrait?' 'That's a self-portrait,' Tomi said. 'O.K.,' I said, 'I just wanted to make sure you heard.' Now take a look at his drawing."

Mr Ungerer, I note, has drawn two hands, one above the other, in each hand there is a penis, one pointing north, the other south, above the north-pointing penis there is the word 'YES', below the south-pointing penis the word 'NO.'

"Well, if that's how Tomi sees himself," Burt Britton says, "you can't argue with that."

Burt Britton is in charge of review copies at the Strand Book Store. Bear in mind that no book gets launched in the U.S. without at least two hundred copies going out, and that most of them come zinging straight in to the Strand, and you start to get some idea of Burt Britton's role. Burt does two main things with these books. He ships huge numbers out to libraries, top libraries, making sure that they're getting the best of what's being published. The other thing he does is, when he gets a book that he thinks might get lost in the shuffle, not get noticed, not get properly reviewed, he phones up reviewers, pushes, presses, and then down to the Strand they come, these influential reviewers, and Burt fills them in. He did this to Gabriel Garcia Marquez's *One Hundred Years of Solitude*, which he read in proof, and was sure wasn't going to get noticed unless he did something. South American books, at that time, were the kiss of death.

In a word, Burt Britton is the powerbroker of books.

I ask him to join me for lunch. "Can't," he says, the phone

49

ringing again behind the mountain of books. "I've got about thirty librarians coming here in about two minutes," he says. "Well, bring them along," I say. It is not every day, understand, that one meets a genuine fan. "These are *librarians*," Burt Britton says gravely, glaring at me. "You wouldn't like them, Morris. These are serious people." O.K., no lunch. We arrange to have dinner the following night. Burt scribbles down his address, then disappears again to answer that endless telephone. I make my way out to the street, on the way buying three more books.

Miles Davis is playing on the stereo when Burt Britton opens his door to me the following night. He ushers me into his apartment, introduces me to Korby, his girl, hands me a glass of Scotch only slightly smaller than my wastepaper basket at home. My head swivels. I am looking at Burt Britton's books.

There are five thousand books here, in this room, maybe ten, possibly more, packed tight on shelves so high you need ladders to get to the top third (yes, there are ladders), books in piles on the floor, books on tables, books on chairs. "Here you are, Morris," says Burt Britton, before I can speak, and hands me a dozen books. "These are for you."

James Salter, Edmund Wilson, Joanna Kaplan, Arnold Wesker, Philip Roth, Jonathan Baumbach, Peter Matthiessen . . . writers I know, writers I don't, review copies, the latest, brand new. "How the hell am I going to shlepp all this stuff home?" I say, exhibiting my celebrated gratitude. "Listen," says Burt Britton, "when I came back from England last year, a little holiday, I had five stacks like that. Five! Hand luggage. The rest was in the cases. Listen, you read Robert Stone? Korby, fetch me a Robert Stone. You like poetry? Korby, bring me a John Hollander, and, let's see, Richard Howard." My stack grows and grows. "Help," I cry in delight. "Are you sure you can spare all this stuff? I mean, have you read them all?" "Read them?" says Burt Britton. "I am," he says, the dark darting eyes looking straight into mine, "the world's greatest reader."

Now, if anyone else made such a claim within my hearing, I would fall about in heaps, but Burt Britton is not kidding. He reads. He has read. He knows everyone. Grace Paley. Joy Williams. Hortense Calisher. Mark Mirsky. Gilbert Sorrentino.

50

would be happy to reciprocate at an

Sincerely,

Jay D. Lussan
Executive Vice President

Normal terms of sale:_____ open

Credit line $_____

Volume w/this acct. last yr. ___ Under

Account is presently:___ Current ___ P

In general, this account:___ takes dis

Is slow by ____ 30 days ____ 60 days __

Do you consider this a desirable accou

Remarks:_____

_____

_____

126 Pacific Ave. • Box 1859 • Aspen, Colo. 81611 • (303) 92

Do you know these people? Burt Britton does. He has read every-one.

"I read my first book," he tells me, "when I was twenty-three years old. William Faulkner. *The Hamlet*. That was the first. Before that I hadn't bothered with books, didn't know what they were all about, didn't care. I was a Marine. Made Sergeant. But what I was interested in, the only thing I was interested in, was baseball. The Dodgers. My Brooklyn Dodgers. You don't know the Dodgers?" Burt Britton looks at me, outraged and sad at the same time. "Morris, you never heard of Robinson and Reeve, Furillo, Campanella, Cox, Snider, Hodges, Erskine, Labine, Gilliam, Podnes, Black, Durocher, Dressen, Stankey, Casey, Ramazotti, Amoros, Rojek, Lavagetto, Hermanski? Morris, you never heard of *Pistol Pete Reiser*! They were my life.

"I became an actor so I could go out to the Coast when the Dodgers moved out there. You know what kind of actor I was? I was George C Scott when they wanted Tab Hunter. That was me in Hollywood. I came back here. That's when I read Faulkner, when I realized what I'd been missing. I had a lot of spare time, being an out-of-work actor, so I got in a lot of reading. I read like crazy. Morris, I had a lot of catching up to do. I was round at the Strand so much they offered me a job, which I resisted at first, I mean, I didn't want to work in a *book store*, but finally I thought, why not? They pay me a lot of money there, Morris, and I get all my books cheap. Stop jumping around, Morris, you're in for a rare treat. I am going to read to you. You know John Sanford? *A More Goodly Country*? Listen."

It has grown dark in this huge book-filled room where we sit. The ceiling has disappeared, the shelves have been swallowed up, become fabulous dark cliffs. Burt Britton puts down his cheroot, picks up a book, opens it carefully, no more than four or five inches, holds it more carefully than I have ever seen a human being holding a book, and then, wonder of wonders, picks up a large silver flashlight, flicks it on, shines it into the valley of print in his hand, and reads.

" 'He came out as you went in' " he reads, " 'and it took your mind a moment to see in the slush downfall of his face the one that once was snow, and by then the door to the hall had stuttered and closed . . .' " F. Scott Fitzgerald. Burt Britton reads it carefully and well, between sentences looking across at me for my reaction. The silver flashlight is steady in his hand. This is not a performance. Burt Britton is sharing his wonder, his pride, his joy.

We stand up to go to dinner. I am almost out of the door when I see Burt doing a quick check of the ashtrays, seeing that nothing is still alight. "There's a lot of paper in this apartment, Morris," he says, drilling me with his eyes. "I noticed," I say. We go out.

2. Foreplay

Any minute now Random House is going to press the button and that will be that. No more. Finito. Curtains. The end. On Burt Britton's face, when he tells me this, is an expression impossible to define — part panic, part celebration, part relief. Plus about nine other parts. The tip of his cheroot glows like a ruby. His eyes dart around, checking the scene. And then they flip back and stare at me, challenging me to speak. I don't say a word.

It's a year later, I am back in New York, back at the Strand, back behind the rope where it says EMPLOYEES ONLY, back in Burt Britton's Everests of Literature basement domain. I take a breath. A column of books begins to sway. "Careful, Morris!" Burt barks, leaping to restore stability. "Christ, you're worse than Zero!"

Whereupon he launches into stories about the unruly behaviour of Zero Mostel, but it is not my task here to retail such salacious gossip — and anyhow there isn't time. Random House's finger is poised over the button . . . the seconds are ticking away . . .

Burt Britton crushes out his cheroot, instantly lights another. He is nervous, tense, "Did I tell you I got Borges?" he shoots out at me, a corner-of-the-mouth whisper, but the news is too great for whispering, his voice rises at once. "Yeah, he came down," he says, "*a blind man*, did a drawing for me, right here!" He darts off, is back in a second with the Borges, a maze of lines, a labyrinth, the only clear thing the signature at the bottom. "I also got George Oppen," he says. "You don't know George Oppen? Morris, what's the matter with you?" He shows me the Oppen. And then he shows me, I forget who he shows me, a dozen people, a hundred, maybe more . . .

"Burt," I say, "what are you doing here? This is not a collection any more! This is not a selected gathering of favourite writers! This is . . . this is an *encyclopedia*!"

Burt Britton ignores this, "Jesus, I am tired, Morris," he says, removing his gold-framed spectacles to give his eyes a rub. "You know what time I got to bed last night? Who I was getting a self-portrait of? Wait'll you hear this . . ."

No less a personage than the famed Spanish poet and playwright Arrabal, is what Burt tells me, he heard he was in town for a couple of days, so he got his address, went there at seven o'clock, straight from the Strand, rung the bell, no one there, went across the street and sat in a bar and every half hour rushed out and tried the doorbell again and it was three o'clock in the morning when he finally got someone, only it wasn't the great Arrabal, it was someone else, this someone else informing Burt that Arrabal was back in Spain, he'd nipped away early, or maybe it was Paris . . .

Burt looks distraught, weary, defeated, crushed . . . but only for a moment. "You know what I got this morning?" he says, back to his corner-of-the-mouth whisper. He bends down and extracts an envelope, an airmail envelope, from the bulging leather shoulder bag he is never more than three steps away from. *"Nabokov,"* he breathes. *"From Monteux."* "Nab?" I say. "The great Nab?" and am about to congratulate him, no one gets to the great Nab, that prince of recluses, when something in Burt's expression tells me that all is not well.

"From *Vera,*" he says, and out of the envelope he slides . . . not an original self-portrait, such as every writer Burt has ever approached has produced without hesitation or qualm, but, from the great Nab, as supervised by his wife, who is said to hold the great Nab as one would hold a diamond in rush hour on Broadway . . . a Xerox copy! And a lousy Xerox at that.

"A Xerox!" thunders Burt. "A stinking Xerox!" He shows it to me. Nab has drawn himself as, well, think about it for three seconds and that's what he's done . . . a butterfly. The minor species butterfly that the Nab himself discovered, just to make the picture complete. With his signature underneath, and the date, and Montreux too. Very pretty. But a Xerox?

"Why has she done this to me?" Burt wails. "What's going on

53

here? Jesus Christ! Listen, I'm writing to her tonight, I don't care, either I get the original or he's not in the book! I'm telling it to her straight. I'm going to tell her Random House have got the finger on the button . . ."

I wish I could tell you how many self-portraits Burt has got, but I can't. The original idea was for Random House to print one per page, but that's out of the question now, it's going to be three per page, and maybe even more. New pages keep getting added all the time. The book is already listed in Random House's catalogue, there's a description, a publication date, a price . . .

Meanwhile Burt is writing to each and every writer in the book, thanking them, making sure he's got permission to print (two writers have died since this began), and he's writing an introduction and having doubts and fears about his prose style (which is terrific) and asking top writers all round the town what they think and then disregarding their advice . . . all this, and working nine or ten hours a day down in the Strand's book-stacked basement, answering the endless phone, browbeating librarians and reviewers, finding rare books for friends, turning people on to what he thinks, *knows,* they can't live another minute without . . . and in between all this, around it and under it and over it, collecting, still collecting, frantically collecting, a collector on a hot tin roof, the guillotine about to fall, Random House's finger trembling over the final button . . .

Burt and Korby and I are sitting with Harold Brodkey, who is probably the nicest man in New York, certainly the nicest writer. We're having a quiet dinner, or what passes for a quiet dinner in the company of the electric Burt, and Harold poses the inevitable question.

"Listen, Burt," he says, "what are you going to do when this book is out of your hands?"

Burt looks instantly jittery. He doesn't know what to say. He doesn't want to *think* about such a thing.

"You can retire, you know," Harold Brodkey says, "I mean, that collection, those drawings, that's a unique thing you've got there. That's for a museum. Those drawings — how many have you got? A thousand? Two thousand? That's fifty thousand dollars!"

"What?" says Burt, whose attention has strayed, as it so often does, he's looking around the restaurant, maybe some truly famous writer has just slipped in, someone who needs to be in the book, a fringe poet, a memoirist, a . . .

"It could go to a quarter million." Harold Brodkey says. "What you've got there . . ."

And suddenly Burt's face lights up, he is all at once the happiest I've seen him this visit, maybe ever.

"A quarter million, Harold?" he says and his glow is unbelievable, a marvel, a joy, he's Einstein clicking onto Relatively, he's Watson and Crick plunging for the double Helix, he's Col. Sanders frying his first chicken . . .

"A quarter million, Harold?" he says again, shedding wattage left and right, but of course he won't sell the drawings, not in a million years, how could he do such a thing to all those writers who have . . . and anyhow, who wants to sell them, who needs the money?

"The Burt Britton Collection," he whispers, and pauses to savour the sound, and each of us smiles, and bows his head, honoured to be in the presence of this arrived Ulysses, this New York *force*. "The Burt Britton Collection."

3. Climax

It's mid-November. I am back in New York. I phone Burt Britton, jet-lag notwithstanding. Our conversation is sharp and to the point. "Come down," he says. "I've got advance copies." Bang! He hangs up. I jump into a cab.

So here I am again, down in the basement at the Strand, back in Burt Britton's sacred domain. Hey, and here's John Ashberry. Here's Donald Windham. Here's Joel Oppenheimer. Here's Howard Moss. Here's Whitney Balliett. Here's Everett Opie. My God, it's an absolute procession, living writers without end, each come at Burt's bidding to collect his gratis copy.

And here is the legendary Burt, worn to a frazzle but not showing it for a second. Between cheroots he tells me that he's written to every single person in the book to make sure he's got permission to use their drawing, then he's written to them all again to express his thanks, and then again, to invite them to the launch party. There are seven hundred and thirty-nine self-portraits in Burt Britton's book. Random House offered to handle the correspondence but Burt wouldn't hear of it, "Those writers did their drawing for *me!*" he shouts. "Their generosity! Their kindness! How could I not write to them personally after they'd done that?"

My head whirls with postage computations, but I agree with Burt, it's the diplomatic thing to do, but let me tell you about this procession. It lasts for two weeks. Right up to the party. Living writers without end. And as each one comes up Burt hands him or her a gratis copy of the book and let me tell you what they do, these living writers, each and every one, without fail. They turn, seemingly nonchalant, the pages, this way, that way, calm, unhurried, only there's nothing calm and unhurried about it. What they're doing, each and every one of them, is *seeing what page they're on!* Are they up the front with the important people? Are they in the middle with the riff-raff? Or, God forbid, down the back with Emergent Nations? More than that, are they in a good position on the page? Have they been printed smudgy or clear? Heavens, they are a curious bunch, these top literary folk!

Actually, Burt has been to great pains to avoid exactly this kind of fuss. He's arranged the drawings in the most incredibly subtle fashion, separating playwrights (who might also be novelists) from poets (who have written short stories), journalists from essayists, illustrators from real artists, and so on, the most logical scramble imaginable, impossible to take offence no matter where you are, unless you're desperate for the very front page, and you can't have that, because that's a drawing of Burt Britton himself, drawn by one John Walker, a Strand employee, and showing Burt standing at Dostoyevsky's grave and tearing his hair.

Everett Opie comes down. Opie works for *The New Yorker*, has been drawing cartoons for them for years. He sits down with his book on an upended box, turns to his page, studies his self-portrait, asks himself, "Do I look like this?" answers, "Yes . . ." asks himself, "Is this a good drawing?" replies, "Not bad . . . hmm . . . yes . . . this is not bad . . . in fact, it's good, very good, yes . . . yes, this is a very good drawing . . ." sits like that for two hours, asking and answering, doesn't look at another drawing in the book, and he'd probably still be there if the Strand didn't throw everyone out at six-thirty every night.

But the party, the party . . .

The party is, of course, at the Strand, where else? The invitation says six-thirty, and the way it has been organised is that Fred Bass, who owns the Strand, has chopped half an hour off his trading day, thirty minutes for Random House to set up the bar, for the staff to get the premises spic and span . . .

But not too spic and span. Which, anyway, would be impossible. I mean, there are tables here, loaded with books, they must weigh, each one, tons and tons, who's going to move all that aside?

Nothing is moved aside. No area has been created in which to dance the tango or swing a cat. Anyhow, top literary folk don't want to do things like that. What they want to do is get themselves a drink, and you couldn't ask for a sturdier bar than the sales counter. Up one end of which, just in case you haven't got one already, are heaped-up stacks of THE BOOK, and right next to them is the cash register. Fred Bass, leave us not forget, is a bookseller, first and last. The music of money punctuates the drinking and talk.

O.K., here I am at last, it's six-forty-five, the greatest literary party in the history of New York is in sway. (*Women's Wear Daily,* tomorrow, will put the number of people here as eight or nine hundred, *The New Yorker,* those sticklers for accuracy, will have it as fourteen or fifteen hundred.) I put one foot in the door and here is Gordon Lish, looking small and grey and wringing his hands and pretending, as is his fashion, that he's not even here, he's just waiting for his wife to arrive so they can go somewhere more important. Before I can get past him he introduces me to Don DeLillo, whose novel, *Ratner's Star,* I unfortunately found unreadable, but I smile, I summon up a nice thing to say, at the same time inching myself and the fabulously beautiful divorcee who is my companion for the evening through the press of people squeezed between the bookladen tables towards the bar . . .

Hey, there's Ralph Ellison!

I pause to pat the shoulder of Harold Brodkey, who is in deep intellectual and philosophical conversation with . . .

Hey, there's Ann Beattie!

The bartender obviously doesn't want me or anyone else hanging around so no one else can get in . . . he pours a good quart of a bottle of Scotch into the most enormous glass . . .

Hey, there's Kurt Vonnegut!

There's Nat Hentoff!

And Ed Koren!

Hey, and Joel Gray!

And —

Wait a minute . . . Joel Gray? Joel Gray hasn't written a book! He's crashed! The bum has crashed the greatest literary party in the history of New York! I am about to become extremely vexed about this when I recall that Korby runs a snazzy little clothing shop on 57th Street, just a hop and a step from Tiffany's, where she's forever inundated by Lady This and Lady That and Jackie Onassis and suchlike persons leaping in to make instant purchase of a gross of cashmere T-shirts to tide them over the weekend, also she knows showbiz people the way Burt knows literary folk and no doubt she let slip to Joel Gray . . .

Hey, there's Donald Barthelme!

Donald Barthelme, Burt told me, was the only writer who, when Burt phoned him to tell him he had copies and when would he like to drop by and pick his up, said "Mail it." I administer to the great Donald a suitable snub.

Whoops, there's Alfred Kazin!

John Ashberry!

Gay Talese!

But where is Burt Britton?

Burt Britton is nowhere in sight.

Never mind, I'll get to him, who's got time for Burt Britton anyhow, this place is crammed with famous literary figures such as who knows when the world or me will ever see in the one place ever again . . .

Hey, there's Rust Hills!

Hugh Nissenson!

Spencer Holst!

Gilbert Rogin!

Ben Raeburn!

William Gaddis!

What! William Gaddis! But Gaddis is a recluse!

No one sees Gaddis! Gaddis doesn't go to the *movies,* never

58

mind literary parties! But here he is, at Burt Britton's party!

I still can't see Burt Britton.

Cameras are popping. The crush is incredible. Famous folk everywhere you try to step. A pretty little blonde girl from *Women's Wear Daily* taps me on the shoulder, pencil poised over her pad, and asks me if I'm famous. I point her in the general direction of Kurt Vonnegut and David Levine.

Where is Burt Britton?

Hey, there's Stanley G Crawford! What, you don't know Stanley G Crawford? Stanley G Crawford wrote *The Log of the S.S. The Mrs Unguentine,* which is an absolutely lovely book, positive magic. Forget about William Gaddis, you know what Stanley G. Crawford has done? He's *trained* up from New Mexico, just to come to the party.

I still can't see Burt Britton . . .

The crowd parts for a moment and along one wall I see a long stretch of canvas, fourteen feet by four or five, maybe even bigger, and along the top it says that everyone of literary or allied accomplishments is invited to draw himself here (felt pens provided), and in a couple of days the canvas is going to be auctioned and the proceeds will go to Channel 13, which is, I think, some kind of Public Service TV thing. I push through to add my visage to this historic tableau, eyes peeled the while for a glimpse of Burt . . .

The reason I'm so desperate to see him, well, one of the reasons, is that Burt confided to me that a certain number of writers bound to be at the party he'd only met once, and some of them never, it'd all been done through the mail (this was when Random House had its finger on the button and the normal Burt Britton method of self-portrait gathering — the personal approach — became inoperative), and what if he snubbed someone, didn't recognise an important figure? I told him to either get drunk or pretend to be drunk, only way to handle a situation like that. "That's the way I figured it," Burt Britton had growled, stern-faced and panicky at the same time, the inevitable cheroot positively smouldering.

But where is he? Maybe he's not here. Maybe, at the last minute, faced with the prospect of so many writers, so many heroes . . .

Impossible!

Let me quote you what Burt Britton says in the introduction to his book. "And then came the obsession: to try to reach, if possible, everyone who had ever given me anything, a poem, a story, a novel, a line even — what I call a gift, for what else is a story from Chekhov, a novel from Faulkner, a line by Camus? No one, if I could find a way to reach them, should be left out. I OWED THEM."

Looking for Burt in this crush of literary people, less than a tenth of whom I recognize, probably half that, there suddenly comes to me a staggering thought.

Burt Britton has read every single person here!

I am bowled over by this realization. And I think, maybe next year, or the year after, certainly some time in the future, there will be a literary party in New York to beat this one, more people, more famous names, but no matter how big it is, no matter how famous and numerous the guests, it won't be the biggest literary party. Not the way this one is. Because this one is special, one of a kind, never to be repeated. New York will never see its like again. For this is a party of love.

And then I see Burt Britton.

I almost don't recognize him. Where's the battered hide vest, the red kerchief, the rolled-up sleeves, the unruly hair? My God, Burt is wearing a jacket, a nice shirt, a Bloomingdale tie! I've never seen such niceness, such neatness. He's dapper, he's spruce, he's spic and span!

But never mind all that, forget about the clothes, it's the inner man I'm interested in here. I mean, how is he *inside*? Is he worried? Is he frantic? Is he nervous? Is he simulating drunkness? Actually intoxicated?

Not for a minute.

Burt Britton, surrounded by writers, writers incalculable, novelists and short-story writers and editors and journalists and cartoonists and illustrators and essayists and reviewers and publishers and poets both blank and rhymed and anthologists and biographers and memoirists and every other kind of talented genius, hack and ink-stained scribe, words without limit, the end of the rainbow, a dream come true . . . Burt Britton is *floating*.

60

4. Afterglow

Will fame ruin Burt Britton?

It's the day after the party, the morning after, about eleven o'clock. I stagger down the stairs to Burt Britton's domain, shaky with the after-effects of those huge glasses of Scotch, the fabulously beautiful wealthy divorcee, the crush of top literary folk. It is the first time I have been to the Strand without the slightest desire to buy a book. That's how shaky. I turn a corner and there is Burt. My heart leaps up a notch.

Good-bye the jacket, good-bye the nice shirt, good-bye the Bloomingdale tie! Good-bye all that niceness and neatness. Burt is the way he always is, the hide vest, the rolled-up sleeves, the red kerchief, the unruliness about the hair, the inevitable foul cheroot. Fame hasn't done a single thing to him. He's unmarked. He's untouched.

And then I see his eyes.

Hey, where's that dark darting look? Where's the piercing stare? Where's the faster-than-lightning frisk-movement forever checking out the scene?

My God, he's gone dreamy.

It's not the old Burt at all.

Before I can speak, he's scribbling me a list — what is this? — sheet after sheet, handing them to me, I try to focus, hey, he's doing me a list of who was at the party, all the names, at the same time he's telling me he's going on TV, on radio, he's a Book of the Month Club Alternative, did I see the write-up he got in *Mademoiselle,* in *Women's Wear Daily,* he's going to be in *The Yorker,* he tells me, and all the time people are coming up and saying what a great party it was, definitely the greatest ever, and he's shaking hands and smiling — Burt *smiling* — and speaking so politely to one and all, this isn't Burt Britton, any minute now he'll be handing out photographs, possibly even kissing babies, it's unnatural, it's bordering on the obscene.

I mean, what's the kid done? Collected together a few drawings, that's all. And here he is, acting like a superstar.

The telephone rings. Burt answers it with a genteel politeness that even in my shaky after-effects state makes me desirous of a good stiff drink.

But listen, don't get me wrong. I am not begrudging him his fame. Not for a minute. Not at all. As Andy Warhol once said, everyone should be famous for a day, and no one deserved his day more than Burt. Deserved it and earned it. But there are complications here, nuances, things to be got into perspective, sorted out.

For a start, this whole self-portrait thing started out as a private business, a hobby, a personal thing, an intimate giving of gifts, and look what's happened to it. *Mademoiselle! Women's Wear Daily!* TV appearances! A Book of the Month Club Alternative, for God's sake!

But O.K., that'll pass, *Mademoiselle* doesn't do the same person two months running unless he's a she with a slinky figure and a string of flashy boyfriends with personal jets, and even then it's not guaranteed, there are bound to be off-periods.

No, much more crucial is Burt's head. I mean, having been kissed by fame, has he been crippled by that fleeting embrace, is he now going to lust after it for evermore?

And what's he got to offer? He's done every living writer (and two dead ones). Generations will have to pass before a new crop emerges. What's he going to do in the interim?

I am getting sad here, brooding about all this.

More people are coming up, more and more, there's smiling and handshaking and that sort of hushed awe that always surrounds a superstar, and yes, oh dear, people are asking Burt what he's going to do next and he's glowing and floating and being so nice it's terrible to behold and he's saying, well, maybe he'll do famous movie directors, or maybe ballerinas, that'd make a great book, or maybe he'll do baseball stars, he's already got . . .

I've lost him.

The Burt Britton I knew, the world's greatest reader, that lover of literature, that frantic devotee of the written word, is no more.

Annihilated.

Destroyed.

And then this happens:

A guy comes up, an absolutely ordinary guy, about thirty years old, maybe thirty-five, and he says, "Pardon me, is there someone called Burt Britton here? They told me upstairs . . ."

Burt looks at him. I look at him. The most ordinary-looking

thirty to thirty-five-year-old-person you've ever seen.

"Yes?" Burt says.

"Oh," says this guy. "Well. I'm looking for a book. It came out about a week ago, maybe two weeks, I'm not sure. They told me upstairs . . ."

"Yes?" Burt says.

"Well," says this guy, this absolutely ordinary guy, looking more absolutely ordinary by the minute, if you can imagine such a thing, "I don't know the name of it, and it's got a sub-title, but I don't know that either . . . Farrar, Straus, I think, did it . . ."

The dreaminess is gone from Burt Britton's eyes, the superstar ambience, the kiss of fame, all gone, gone instantly, just like that.

"What?" he thunders. "What? How dare you!" he shouts, "Jesus Christ! You don't know the name! You don't know the sub-title! You come down here wasting my time! Get outta here! Go on! Beat it! Scram!" He is shaking, boiling in the face, practically swallowing his cheroot. I have heard Burt berating librarians for mispronouncing Nabokov but never anything like this.

And the absolutely ordinary guy? He's gone white, he's stunned, he's opening and closing his mouth by way of apology but nothing is coming out, he's retreating backwards . . .

"And listen," Burt shouts after him, "on the way out, look under Stevens!" He points with his cheroot. "Over there!"

What? What's this Stevens? There are four or five of us here, fans, Strand employees, writers, I don't know. We stare at Burt, we stare at the retreating absolutely ordinary guy. We see him scanning the shelves, reaching up, taking down a book . . .

"I've got it," we hear him call. "Thank you very much."

He didn't know the title, he didn't know the sub-title . . . I stare at Burt.

"You arranged that," I say. "You set that up. You planned the whole thing. No one can do a thing like that —"

The world's greatest reader fixes me with his dark darting eyes.

"He said Farrar, Straus, didn't he?", he says. "You heard him say that? Farrar, Straus have only done one book this week with a subtitle. It had to be that." If he smiles I don't see it. "Come on," he says, "out of the way. I've got work to do here." A fresh cheroot appears in the mouth. "Jesus, look at this mess," he says. "It's gonna take a month to clean this up." The telephone rings. Burt has grabbed it before the second ring. "Yes!" he barks.

WEIGHTY MATTERS

Here Comes The Apple Man

This is a human-interest story filled with suffering and poverty and flinty-hearted readers are advised to turn the page.

It starts a couple of years ago, not long after we'd moved from London to this village, which is forty-five miles from town. Very quaint. Duck pond, historic church, village green etc. Our house is new, built by an architect for fun and profit, and it stands in what was once an orchard. Very old trees. We've got six apples (five cookers and one eater) and a pear.

Now, I am (or used to be) a city man and look askance at anything that isn't cellophane wrapped, comes in a can, or in a bright packet or box, and when apples and pears started to fall all over our lawn, I got busy with a rake and began to pile them onto the rubbish heap.

I mean, these were windfalls, not the really good apples and pears which were still hanging up in the trees.

Suddenly a strange chap appeared.

When I say strange, I mean he was elderly, over six feet tall, very pale, somehow frail, and moved awkwardly, like a kind of robot.

"Nice apples," he said.

"I don't know what to do with them," I said. "They're falling all over the place."

"I like apples," he said, giving me a strange smile.

"Help yourself," I said.

"Do you mind if I come back with a basket?" he asked.

"Be my guest."

He was back ten minutes later, and I helped him fill his basket.

67

I must have put too many in, because he could hardly lift it. But somehow he did, and staggered off in his strange robot-like way, telling me I was very kind and he'd look after me.

Half an hour later he was back, bearing two huge cabbages.

About a week later I saw him looking sheepishly through our gate. He was eyeing the new load of windfalls that littered the front lawn.

"Come in and help yourself," I told him, and this time helped him fill two baskets.

He staggered off, and then came back with potatoes, carrots, and two more cabbages.

"Hey, you don't have to give me anything," I told him, but he wouldn't hear of it.

He was diabetic, he told me, and for six months of the year practically lived on apples.

"When I can get them," he said, "And you've been very kind."

For the next two months he was around twice a week, taking away apples (I was giving him the good ones now — we had more than enough), and bringing us cabbages and carrots and onions and potatoes and beans.

Which should have been a pretty nice arrangement (we were up to our ears in apple sauce and apple pies and apple chutney and apple tarts and apple everything you can name), but somehow it made me sad to see this strange-looking man staggering up our drive with his cabbages and beans.

I mean, he was a pensioner, probably nearly seventy, and certainly not a well man.

Whenever I saw him in the street, he'd give me a smile and a wave.

"How's your apples?" he'd say.

And then just like that we were out of apples. Finished. Gone.

I saw our apple man in the street. Now here's the strange part. The second he saw me he looked away.

Eight or nine months went past and I hardly saw him at all. And never got a wave out of him, or a smile.

And then apples started to fall again and back he came, with his baskets and cabbages and friendly smile.

It was just like the first year, and when he'd collected the last apple of the season, he was gone again.

He lives just down the end of our street. I went there once. He wanted to show me his vegetables. He had them laid out in neat rows, clusters of onions hanging up in a shed, sacks of potatoes stacked by one wall, more cabbages than you've ever seen in your life.

He lives with his wife in a tiny cottage which is very neat but has that smell of poverty about it you have to experience to understand.

There are a lot of pensioners in this village and they all grow vegetables. Not as a hobby. Not to fill in time. This is how they stay alive. They couldn't do it just on the pension. Their cabbages and their potatoes are a serious business.

Some of them have got them growing in their front gardens as well. Rows and rows of cabbages, thick plots of potatoes, tall stands of runner beans.

You can get an allotment from the council if you don't have enough land of your own. A fair number do that.

Our apple man is lucky. He's got a large garden. But he's also very sick, and has to go to the hospital for treatment quite often.

About three months ago I saw a hearse going down the street. I didn't see where it stopped, but I knew in my bones it was our apple man. I hadn't seen him about for months, and the last time I'd seen him he'd looked terrible, frailer and paler and more awkward than ever before.

It was cold. The cold is what kills pensioners off in this country. They can't afford to buy fuel.

I sat and thought about him, about how he'd been so scrupulous in his trading, and the reason he'd never said hello to me or smiled or waved when we were out of apples was obvious. He'd been terrified I'd asked him for cabbages.

O.K., now let's have a happy ending. Our apples and pears have started falling all over our lawn again. We've got apples and pears all over the place.

And who's that looking in my gate?

Hey, it's our apple man, smiling and waving and coming up the drive in his awkward robot-like way.

Where are our baskets?

"Help yourself!" I tell him. "Come back for more!"

There'll be cabbage for dinner tonight.

Something Beautiful Is Going To Happen

Forty kids, fifty, maybe sixty, I don't know exactly how many, a *lot*, are standing in a line in Central Park, hanging onto huge balloons. Pink balloons and yellow balloons. The yellow ones are about three feet across, the pink a good five. Helium filled. Bobbing. Straining to go free. About a hundred all told, fifty yellow, fifty pink, all the balloons somehow tied to each other with string and the kids just standing there, hanging on, in a neat line.

It's Sunday, round three o'clock. All week it's been sweltery, tropical, to step out of an airconditioned building into the street was to die, New York at its worst, but yesterday it broke, cooled, cleared, a blue-skied absolutely flawless day, a miracle, a joy, and today it's doing something else, I don't know what, one minute it's sunny, the next it's positively chilly. A wind springs up from nowhere, grabs at the line of balloons. A couple of the yellow ones pop. The entire line sways. But the kids are hanging on there, holding tight. The wind drops away, as suddenly as it came. I can feel the kids relax. Whew.

But what's going on?

What's all this with the balloons?

Whatever it is, it is happening, I should tell you, in the midst of an appreciable crowd — a hundred yellow and pink helium-filled huge balloons standing in line is not a common occurrence, it seems, not even in New York . . . all manner of people are standing about, or walking slowly past, or sitting on the grass: artist-type people (heavily into denim) and intellectual-type people (denim plus pipes) and Puerto Ricans and blacks and even a goodly sprinkling of what look like plain family folk, some with

71

kids. Right on cue a little French kid runs past with a squeaky toy on the end of a string.

A typical New York Central Park Sunday crowd.

Except for this balloon business.

Oh, I forgot to mention — most of the kids hanging onto the balloons are wearing bright orange T-shirts, which they're wearing sort of pulled over whatever else they've got on . . . and now that I'm getting a bit more used to the scene, I see that a lot of other people are wearing bright orange T-shirts too — there goes an artist-type girl (denim plus no bra and a certain way about the hair), and there go two intellectual-type persons (though only one has a pipe, the other settling for a stogie) with the orange pulled over . . .

What is *happening* here?

Nothing seems to be happening, is what. Just the kids standing in line with those balloons.

Ten minutes like that. Twenty.

Should I go away?

Wait a minute, there's movement, there's activity. Someone's saying something to the kids through a kind of megaphone, I can't make out the words, he's too far away, pointing the wrong way . . . and look, the line of balloon-bearing kids is starting to travel, guys and girls in orange running around and telling them what to do, where to go —

Hey, they're forming a circle. A perfect circle. On a large smooth flat grassy section just down from where I'm standing. And when they've got it exactly right, the front kid and the back kid standing side by side, there's another message through the megaphone . . . and everyone sits.

I sit too.

Let me look around.

Let me try to figure out exactly what is going on here.

More movement, more activity.

Now the people in orange are swooping down on the circle of balloon bearers and they're all holding these bright green things and when they get to the kids they crouch down and start doing something—

Streamers!

They're attaching green streamers to the circle of bobbing

balloons. Tying them up to the string. And then, the green streamers securely attached, running out from the circle and letting them unravel until what we've got here is green streamers radiating out from the circle like the spokes of a wheel, each one fifty feet long. "Here," says someone to me and hands me an end. Hey, I'm attached to this incredible thing, whatever it is! As are about or at least fifty other people, all of us hanging onto the ends of these green streamers.

Whoops, another wind! Hold tight!

O.K., we've finished with the green, now comes — Pink streamers! Attached to the circle in exactly the same way, a pink between two greens, so what you've got is one pink, one green, another pink, another . . .

More things are happening, different things. Really hectic activity is suddenly taking place, the orange people are swooping down now with flashing squares of something . . . Mylar! Mylar is this unbelievably tough plastic impossible to tear and coated with, I don't know what, but it gleams like silver foil, like a mirror . . . they've got these foot square pieces of Mylar and they're stapling one piece every six feet up and down the pink streamers.

This is getting complicated.

Now the guy with the megaphone is ordering the attachment of large orange streamers to the balloons. These orange streamers are being held, in the roll, unravelled, by yet more people, somehow squeezed between the balloonists.

A Puerto Rican kid is standing next to me. An orange-garbed girl dashes past, with Mylar, staple gun, spare streamers, all manner of things.

"Miss!" shouts the kid. "Miss!"

The girl stops. She turns. Her eyebrows go up.

"Why are you doing this?" says the Puerto Rican kid. There is no humour in his voice. He wants to *know*.

The girl suddenly stops looking busy, her face relaxes, she looks all at once . . . devoted, transported . . .

"Something *beautiful* is going to happen," she says. "In about another five minutes." And off she runs, busy as a bee.

Ah, now I see it, now I know what's what.

I am witnessing, participating in . . . An Event! A Happening! Conceptual Art!

In just five more minutes this whole thing is going to lift up into the blue, the streamers streaming and the Mylar flashing and the balloons . . . which you might not think is a very valid way to make art, because, well, in about ten minutes, fifteen at the most, the thing will have disappeared, been swallowed up by the blue, ceased to exist, vanished, *gone!* which is a thing that, for instance, the Mona Lisa never does, so one of them has to be a fake, right? except, well, this thing that is about to loft up is going to exist forever and ever in our minds, our past, our history, and surely old Mona does exactly the same . . .

"Get ready," says the guy with the megaphone. "Stand up everyone! Stand up! Stand up!"

The kids stand. I stand. Everyone is standing.

"Now, when the balloons go," says the megaphone, "I want everyone holding a streamer to run in towards the middle, O.K.?"

We're ready, we're waiting. Seconds to go.

"Let go! Let go! Let go! Let go! Let go! Let go!" the megaphone chants.

And up go the balloons and in we run and up she goes —

Look —

It's like a sea anemone! like a jellyfish! going up so high so fast it's unbelievable . . . in what seems like only seconds the colours have faded, you can't see the pink, the yellow, it's just a shape, a drifting, rising, slowly changing shape . . . a harp, a heart . . .

A 747 zooms past this apparition in the sky, this already tiny thing . . .

Four o'clock. It's over. That's it. That's all. I ask an orange-garbed person who organized this thing, how long did it take to get together, things like that, and the answer is it's the work of one Jim Thompson, an art instructor at a university in Fresno, California. Work started at one o'clock this afternoon, using mostly volunteers.

"And who paid for it?" I ask.

"Oh, Jim did," he tells me. "It's all out of his own pocket. He's done them before. Actually, I think he's planning another one for later this year."

Out of his own pocket. The balloons, a hundred balloons, at five, ten dollars apiece. Another five or ten apiece for a hundred

74

T-shirts. Mylar is a dollar a square. Two hundred of those, And streamers, miles of streamers, and . . .

The event wasn't photographed, wasn't filmed. No record. Just up and away.

I walk home, across the park, looking up. The thing in the sky is so tiny now it's like one of those motes that floats across the surface of the eye. Maybe that's what it is. Maybe what I'm looking at isn't even there.

Place

My mother knew about Hitler before you. This was in Bialystock, in Poland, '33, '34. They packed their bags — my mother, her mother, two brothers, two sisters. The documents of travel, the visas, the passports, the permissions to leave, the permissions to enter, gathered these precious scraps of paper with lies, with favours, with forgeries, with bribes — God only knows how it was done in those days. But done. Passage booked. America! One final thing: the silver samovar buried under the house. Because they planned to go back one day? So the goyim wouldn't get it, my mother said. Her eyes still angry, twenty years later. America! But the day before they were to sail, a complication. My mother's mother had scars on her lungs. Old scars, nothing, how could it matter, such a thing? It mattered. There was a rule, a law. America was closed. Leave me, my mother's mother said. I will come later. I will find a way. No. Where one went, they all went, all or nothing. A day before. The smell of Hitler's ovens already filled my mother's nose. There was no later.

So where can we go? my mother asked.

A day before.

Australia.

Australia had no law about lungs.

She called it, in the twenty years of our life together, and certainly before that, from the moment she stepped off the ship, in her twenties, a frightened girl, a foreigner for the first time in her life, Australia was always the same to her, a *shreckliceh medineh* — a dreadful society. Why? Because she didn't speak the language? She learnt. Because she didn't know its ways? She

77

learnt. She managed. She married. She brought up a family. She did business. She owned a house. It made no difference. Dying of cancer my mother said it again, it was in her eyes, as it had always been there, the fear, the fright, and see? she had been right, look what it had done to her, this *shrecklicheh medineh.* I stared, speechless. But something else too. Around her eyes there was a softness, a darkness, and I saw there, as I had seen for twenty years, in hints, in whispers, that other place, snow, forests, cobbled streets, that life she had never left, the real place.

I bought luggage. I boarded a ship.

There is a poem by Nabokov, that exile, that emigre, called *An Evening Of Russian Poetry*, and there is the poet, a magician performing to a rapt audience, delighted and delightful, happy, I suppose, clothed, fed, anyhow safe from tyranny, lecturing in America, but suddenly he says

> once in a dusty place in Mora county
> (half town, half desert, dump mound and mesquite)
> and once in West Virginia (a muddy
> red road between an orchard and a veil
> of tepid rain) it came, that sudden shudder,
> a Russian something that I could inhale
> but could not see

and your heart sags.

But Nabokov knew what was gone and what did I have? A hint, a whisper, a darkness around the eyes. The frailest clues. Which seemed enough, certainly in those first years, rushing around Europe, each day as giddy in the legs as though I'd just quit my ship, I rocketed, I raced, by bus, by train, and added, each night, alone in this hotel, that room, another inch of black to the bright-coloured map spread out on my trembling knees. I have been here! And here! And, yes, many times, I felt that sudden shudder, that *something*, I felt it in Paris, in Vienna, in Berlin.

Felt it.

But then it went.

What was it? Was it good coffee, good newspapers, cafe life, walking along boulevards lined with trees? Paris was Hemingway and Gertrude Stein, Berlin was Isherwood, Vienna was Harry Lime. Other places, other things. But underneath all that, yes, still, a different shudder, a different something.

78

Should I go to Poland, to Bialystock, scratch in the soil for my mother's buried silver? Sufficient sanity prevailed to tell me: Don't.

But still that *something*.

Analyse it. Hold it still. What was its composition, its structure, its shape? It seemed to do with mountains, with mist — but it wasn't Switzerland, I looked there — and in my seventh year in Europe I suddenly saw it clearly, plunging from a bright highway down an unlit road, there it was, rising up around me, cliffs of darkness, forms of soft black, the night sky was part of it too, cliffs and caves of cloud low and high, I felt that sudden shudder, and for the first time I held it still, I analysed it, I knew where it was, the real place at last. It was when I was seventeen, a holiday, the first time I had gone anywhere alone, where I awoke each morning to mountains all around, clouds trapped in the trees (it took them half the day to make their escape), and water dripping, water rushing, the sound of wet gravel, the smell of green air.

Seventeen.

In Australia.

I repacked my bags.

I went back.

I am here now.

In Australia.

But no happier.

As uncomfortable as before.

But this is an uncomfortable place. It has always been uncomfortable. Long before Hitler. Long before Bialystock. Look at the first paintings ever done of this land. The sky is the backdrop of a touring company melodrama. The virgin bush is the Kew Gardens. The natives are Boy's Own adventure tales. The eye sees what it has been schooled to see, fed by Culture, fed by Education, fed by Social Life, and no one was prepared for *this*. The painter's discomfort booms from the canvas.

But these were Englishmen, far from Home, rushed for time. Let there be time. There was. A first generation born here, ignorant of anywhere else. Then a second, firmer still. This generation opened its eyes and what it saw was Light. Australian Light. They made that discovery. Australian Light is not like European Light.

They founded a School of it. Painting after painting. And good paintings, some of them. Real. That's how it *looks*. He's got it *exactly*, he's got it *right*. But the painter is still outside, the mechanics mastered, that five-finger exercise, but what else? What do you do with it? What happens now?

(My mother closed her eyes, made tea, sat in her darkened kitchen, moaned, sipped her tasteless tea.)

We have new painters, we have Sidney Nolan, Fred Williams, a whole host of new painters, but there is something about those two. Nolan. His vast skies. His twisted trees. His sun-bleached grass. Yes. There is that instant recognition. Nolan's paintings could be nowhere else on earth. But is it here? Because Nolan is more than real, more than how it really is. He is what we want to believe about this land *now*. Nolan paints the new, the latest, myth.

Fred Williams touches the target nearer the heart. He has the twisted trees, the vast skies, the sun-bleached grass, yes, all that, but something else too. His is the vital something, and what it is is omission. His landscapes stretch empty as far as the eye can see. He paints the endless curvature of the earth. But empty. There are no people. This is Australia, where man has made no mark.

(I went, a boy, to the National Gallery, other galleries, and come home, boiling with paint, and spread out my brushes on the dining room table, my papers, my saucers of pigment, and was about to begin — had already begun, inside my head the paintings were already there — when my mother clapped a hand to her heart. Europe spoke. Painters starve! I packed away my undreamed dreams.)

The country. The essence of the country. No people. Man has made no mark. Because he hasn't been here long enough? Too easy to answer. Not really an answer at all. The real answer is uncomfortable. We are uncomfortable here. And always will be. The secret of survival is: Recognize that.

But the cities? What about the cities? Forget the cities. The cities are nothing. The cities are vain echoes of any place you've ever been. You can feel the homesickness, the longing, the lostness. English Colonial. Spanish Style. Italian Influence. Scandinavian Open Air. They rise and fall, to the pulse of migration, to the fashion of the day. The coups are endless and bloodless. Why should there be blood? There is no blood here. The cities are transparent veneers peeling endlessly under the sun.

Futile dreams.

So what is it, this Australia? A refuge for scarred lungs? Someone asked me once to write about Australian Jewish humour. There are a lot of Jews here, anyway enough. Communities. Synagogues. A history of Jews. I thought about it. I listened. I watched. I couldn't. There isn't any. Because how can you laugh when at any minute the scars could break, revealing — what? It could be anything. Don't take a chance. Be quiet. Be still. Get on with your business. Just like everyone else.

Yes, true, all of it, there is nothing else to say.

Except this.

I sat, one day, with my wife, my English wife, in the country. We ate. We drank. The children played in the grass. Then my wife, my English wife, looked around, looked at the trees that are not really trees, and the rocks that are not really rocks, the green is not green, the bark, the shapes are wrong, and at the wrong earth, and at the wrong sky, and she said, "If I ever left here, I would miss this place."

Violence On Upper Broadway,
New York City, USA

A man is being thrown out of a supermarket on Upper Broadway, between Ninety-seventh and Ninety-eighth. A black man. Well, I think it's a black man. I can't see too well. Actually, I'm not trying to see at all, I'm not sure I want to know anything about it, I'm just standing here at the checkout counter trying to pay for orange juice, cashew nuts and milk, except the girl at the register is not taking any notice of me, she's swung around, she's craning to see what's going on. Desperate to see. Mouth open, eyes positively jumping.

There's a way of walking down a street here, and I don't mean just Upper Broadway, which is semi-tough, or anyway a carnival, something happening all the time, panhandlers, weirdos, freaks, drunks and derelicts, the turned-on and turned-off, I mean any street, Fifth Avenue, Park Avenue, Fifty-seventh Street, the Tiffany's part of town, Sak's, Dunhill's, the gorgeous stores, the plush hotels. You don't look at anything. You keep your eyes down. You mind your own business. Hurry past. And this is not just advice for tourists, this is how New Yorkers go too. Sneak a look around and you'll see that's what everyone's doing. Everyone locked tight in his private world.

I stand with my orange juice, cashew nuts and milk. The girl at the register is taking absolutely no notice of me, doesn't even know I exist, I could probably walk out with the stuff. But I don't. What's going on here? Whatever it is, it's happening behind a tall stand, over in a corner, I can't see a thing. But I can hear plenty: shouting, cursing, scuffling sounds. The girl at the cash register stands up, on her toes. A black girl, very pretty. There are a lot of black people around here, a lot of Puerto Ricans. Spanish Harlem is not far away, creeping down all the time.

You keep your eyes down in New York, as I've said, but it's hard. For instance, near the subway entrance at Ninety-sixth Street, just down from it there's a newsstand, and next to the newsstand, day and night, just about any hour you can name, there's always a crowd. Usually it's a con game, you know, a guy deals out three cards on top of a box and you're invited to guess what card is there, it looks easy, money is changing hands all over the place, fives, tens, big wads, everyone's winning, except half the winners, maybe all of them, are ring-ins, drumming up trade, or trying to, and everyone else is just looking, standing around, hoping to see some sucker fleeced, or just enjoying the carnival atmosphere, women with shopping bags, kids, sports of all sorts, and then suddenly it erupts, there's pushing, there's shouting, tempers flare, someone's got annoyed, and that's when you drop your eyes, that's when you get out of there. But it's hard. You'd like to stay and watch. You don't.

What *is* happening here? The shouting and pushing and scuffling has got really wild. The girl at the cash register is breathing through her mouth, hard. Now she's jumping out from behind the register, she wants to see. I put down my orange juice, cashew nuts and milk. I'm not going to get served here for a while, that's for sure. I take a few steps in the direction of the commotion, but carefully, warily. I don't want to get into anything here.

Tempers flare quickly in this city. Everything's a crisis. The air is electric, volatile, one spark, you feel, and up it'll go. A couple of times I've seen what I was sure was going to be violence, real violence, but both times it didn't happen. The shouting was unbelievable, the cursing, the taunts, and then it just stopped, stopped dead, that was all, that was it, and both times what stopped it was wit. New York wit. "You change your underpants and I'll change mine!" a man yells at a cab driver who has almost run him down. The cab driver scowls, but smiles too, acknowledging the snappy repartee. A bus driver is about to murder a man who has got on without paying. "I'm going to visit with my mom, what do ya want from me?" the man shouts. "*You* got a mom?" the bus driver says. "Jeez." The bus laughs, applauding the performance, the volcano subsides.

84

But it's not subsiding here. This is real violence. I take another step. It *is* a black man. I don't know what he's done or what he's accused of having done but here he is, being thrown out of this supermarket. Really being thrown out. He's going out backwards, trying to say something, explain, but not getting a chance. Someone is pushing him, two people, maybe more. And someone else is running around and shouting. Really shouting. This is not New York wit that's being shouted here. This is real shouting. "You black bastard! You ever come in here again I'll kill ya! Get outta here!" A white-haired guy, in his sixties. The owner, Spanish. Spit flying from his mouth, furious. What has this black guy *done*, for God's sake?

That New York is violent is an old story, everyone knows about it, every visitor comes back with his own favourite story, but this should be understood: the guy who mugs you is not being violent for the sake of violence, it's got nothing to do with the electric air, nothing like that. The muggers of New York, ninety-nine times out of a hundred, are doing it because they want a fix. Junkies. Desperate for the ten dollars that'll see them through the night. They don't want your jewels, your traveller's cheques, your Bankamericard. Give them the ten dollars and you'll both be O.K. Everyone in New York understands that. It's a fact of life. Cab drivers always have ten or twenty dollars stashed away, mugger's money, they give it up on the spot. One of the prices you pay for living in the city. Dickie Wells, the trombonist, didn't have a cent on him when he was mugged. He's in hospital, badly cut up. Don't fool with muggers. Pay them the ten. Except that's changing too. A while ago a lady on the Upper East Side decided not to hand over the ten but to scream instead and what happened was people started coming out of the woodwork, all those New Yorkers who look away and never hear anything and don't want to know what's happening if it's not happening to them, out they came, and then the cops came, and just in time too. The good people of New York were beating that mugger to death.

"O.K., O.K.," the black guy is saying, or trying to say, "I'm going," but that doesn't seem to be enough. The owner keeps up his shouting, worse than before, really furious, and the other guys, the ones who are doing the pushing, are getting more violent. One in particular, in a tight brown suit, is doing most of the work. Out of the door they go, the whole lot of them, shoving and shouting and the black man still moving backwards, out into the street.

Forget the orange juice, the cashews, the milk. I am out in the street too. So is the cash register girl. So is everyone. Just like that the street is crowded, people everywhere. Eyes down is not the rule any more. Everyone's watching, open mouthed.

The feeling you get in New York all the time is that any minute a steel hand is going to pluck you out of the crowd and that'll be that. It's like a lottery, every time you walk down the street. Maybe you'll make it, maybe you won't. The black guy hasn't made it. And you can't help thinking, an appalling thought: good. That means my chances are better for a while. You don't want to think it, but it's there, that loathesome thought.

The man in the brown suit is getting really mean now. He's kicking the black guy. Once, twice, piston kicks, streetfighter stuff, ghetto techniques, no expression on his face as his foot lashes out, gets the black guy in the stomach, between the legs. The black guy looks astounded, stops, once again opens his mouth to speak. The man in the brown suit smiles, the coldest smile you've ever seen, a Richard Widmark smile, and then he makes a little movement. He flips his hand in under his jacket. Everyone in the street knows what that movement means. He's got a knife in there. He's daring the black guy to try something. The black guy shakes his head. The man in the brown suit kicks him again.

Violence in New York is an old story, it's part of the image New York projects to the outside world, as real as the Empire State Building, it's real as that, a tangible feature of the town, but look at the faces, here on Upper Broadway, the women, the children, the weirdos, the sports, look at their faces watching this black guy getting kicked. Hanging mouths, staring eyes. They're horrified. They don't know what to do. The fabric of life in this city might be thin, but at least it's a fabric, it's something, and here, before their eyes, it's being ripped apart. This is real violence. Their faces are powerless. They don't know what to do. This isn't just New York any more, this is any city, anywhere, when the ground slides out from under your feet. Right this minute, right now, New York is no tougher than anywhere else.

Sirens are wailing. Two police cars, a riot van, lights spinning

on top. Just like that there are cops all over the place. I can't
see what's happening any more. People are starting to walk away.
Someone makes a joke.

You Can Go Home Again

Afternoon. Two o'clock. Warm sun. Tenuous breeze. The muffled rub of tyres on the main road at the end of the street comes to me like the sound of the sea. Sandcastles. Waves. A schoolbell rings. Children — my son and daughter amongst them — rush out to play and I can practically smell the sea in their sudden freedom, their noisy joy. Brakes squeal on the main road. A backing truck drills the day. I am not at the sea. I am in my workroom, the room where I come every day to write.

I light a cigarette.

It is a small room. It has a table, a chair, a bed (which I don't use), a mirror, a chest of drawers. Where once a fireplace used to be there is a grey gas heater, and over it, on the mantlepiece, are three framed pictures (cut out of magazines) of frisky Airedales, black and white. I didn't put them there and I won't take them away. A window, a door. The door leads to a kitchen (which I also don't use), and from the window the view is of flowers (hydrangeas, carnations), a small tree. Six or eight feet from the window there is a high wooden fence, and almost directly behind that the brick side of a new block of flats. Ugly. Louvered windows. Wrought iron. A slice of red-tiled roof. It is a limited view, it is almost no view at all, but it suits me fine. I am wary of views, and in Lindos, on the isle of Rhodes, where my room had a view of the columns of the ancient Acropolis, sea to the left, the blue bay of St Paul to the right, and in between the white, close-packed houses of the village, roofs, donkeys, arches, cats, the church bell tower, the narrow cobbled streets, I turned my table away and sat facing a blank white wall. In Copenhagen I had a view of grey slate roofs and shuttered windows (which opened from time to time on scenes of quiet Danish domesticity: a woman walking a baby, a man reading a newspaper in an old faded armchair), in Tangier I looked out at palm trees and the sea, in London my first room faced a gasometer and a rusted car. (The car had no wheels and sat in a yard of weeds.) In nine years I have worked in a dozen rooms at least, rooms all over Europe and two in North Africa, rooms where birds swooped in over my head (Lindos again), where the wind rattled the shutters and slammed the door (Mykonos), where lift machinery whirred just outside my window and drove me mad (Madrid), a beautiful room in Buckinghamshire with a black-beamed ceiling where I wrote on a long refectory table looking out through a conservatory at cows and hills, and when it snowed the conservatory changed shape, became low and dark, lit by a strange light. But all work-rooms are essentially the same, somewhere quiet where I can go about the business of explaining my life, or versions of it, and this room is like every other room I have sat in, thought in, paced, except for one thing. This room is in Melbourne. I was born in this city. In this room, for the first time in nine years, I am no longer an expatriate.

It is a curious feeling.

I swore, of course, never to return. Which is what expatriates do. Otherwise, what are you? A tourist. What a shallow word! I was twenty-six when I left. I remember that last morning. An intensely pretty girl drove me to the ship. Luggage. Crowds. Up the gangplank, feeling foolish. What a performance. I didn't want any of this. I just wanted to slip away, to be gone. The rails were thronged, so was the wharf. Those first inches of water in between. There were some Italians there, I remember, who had made a kind of streamer out of stockings, knotted them together, and as the ship moved out it stretched and stretched to an incredible length, and when it snapped there was a cheer. Shouts. Tears. The crowd on the wharf waved itself into a blur. Water widened. But the rails remained packed, everyone straining for one last look, craning for a final picture. I pushed away. There was nothing there I wanted to see. I had done it at last. Left. Escaped. It was a Greek ship, and I went below for my first European lunch. Five weeks later I was in Europe, an expatriate at last, a true expatriate . . . staying with old Melbourne friends.

Out of one bubble and into another. For six months I lived in what is known in the novels as an "expatriate colony," in beautiful Lindos, on the isle of Rhodes. Englishmen and Americans, some Swedes, a Dutch couple, my Melbourne friends, and me. We were painters and sculptors and writers and poets, just like in the novels. The writers didn't write and the sculptors didn't sculpt and once when I sneaked into the studio of a painter (a secretive man who went off to work every day), I saw that all he had done in four years was paint small circles. Wobbly circles. But that's another story, first bubble first.

My parents were born in Europe, in Poland, and came here in the thirties, my father by way of Israel, or Palestine as it was then, where he lived for seven or eight years. I have a photograph of him squatting in the dust at the quarry in Jerusalem where he worked, a broadshouldered young man with cheeky eyes. He was happy there, it was the best period of his life, he used to tell me again and again. He rode a motorcycle, he danced, he got drunk, he swam in the sea, and he came here in the early thirties because for two years in Palestine there had been no work, he had sat around with nothing to do, he had got depressed. He intended to stay here for only one year, save his money, go back, but he never did. Lonely, alone, all his friends and family over there, he met my mother and in less than a year they were married. She was from the same city in Poland, I suppose that was a bond, but he hadn't known her there. My father never spoke of Poland. Palestine was his past.

My mother, on the other hand, had everyone, her parents, her sisters and brothers, a close circle of old Polish friends, and it was into this strange world that I was born. She had made a bubble for herself, you see, a curious bubble out of which she never stepped. Poland didn't exist any longer, not her Poland, but neither did Australia. She refused to acknowledge its existence. Australia was this unfortunate thing that history had done to her and her family. It was possible to live here, it was even possible to do very well, but it had no "life", it was a strange, alien, incomprehensible place. All her life here my mother looked out at it, this "new society" as she called it, a mocking tone to her voice, suspicious, wary, but not really wanting to know, not interested, a little, I suppose, like an animal peering through the bars of its cage. Except that she had built the cage. And I lived in there with her, looking out through the same bars. She spoke quite often of Poland with her family and friends, in Polish, usually, which I don't speak (this was the language she used when she didn't want me to eavesdrop, and for even more private matters she fled to Russian), and when I asked her what it was like there, her answer was always the same: "You wouldn't understand." But I picked up the hints and whispers, the deep forests, the laughter, the gossip, joy in the snow. When I left, at twenty-six, I wasn't becoming an expatriate. I was going home.

But I am mistrustful of those people who can give you exact reasons for their actions, crisp, hard balance sheets, impeccable logic, cut and dried. Was my mother's bubble the real reason I left? Why didn't I listen to my father and go to Israel instead? Why didn't his history stir me inside, the way my mother's did?

But Hemingway went to Europe, so did Scott Fitzgerald, Henry Miller, Gertrude Stein, E E Cummings, John Dos Passos, Ezra Pound. I wanted to be a writer too. Europe was where you had to go. Europe had culture, history, it was the beacon. Everything good had come from Europe, and in Australia had been watered down, lost its energy, its vitality, become at best second-rate. Just look at my mother's eyes when she spoke about Europe, and she knew nothing about writers and writing, she had never heard of Hemingway or Fitzgerald or Ezra Pound or Gertrude Stein.

And another thing. (Was this the real reason? was this why I left?) I was twenty-six-years-old and had never done a thing. I walked around in a heavy black overcoat made up of doubts and fears, wrong turnings, hesitations, failures, losses of nerve, a coat so thick and heavy I could hardly move, and in Europe I might still have it but no one would see it for what it was. I could pretend to be wearing something else.

(But what about those Melbourne friends, waiting for me in Lindos? Well, they had their coats too. We could all pretend together.)

Reasons, reasons.

And then there was the business of my brother, my younger brother. When my parents died we moved into a flat together, two bachelor boys, except that I was suddenly a father and a mother as well, and I'm not saying that we didn't have great times, but all I could see was an endless tunnel, no light at the end, and

92

after a year of it I left him with an uncle and boarded that ship. "I have to go," I told my brother. "I can't explain it. I just have to go."

In Lindos the first story I wrote was about a young writer who discovered every day in what he had written the day before lines of Hemingway and Scott Fitzgerald and Dylan Thomas and Mark Twain, and one day he woke up on the floor and saw his table covered with paper and when he sorted it out he saw that he had written William Golding's *Lord of the Flies*, word for word, right down to the punctuation, a perfect copy, not a single mistake.

A Melbourne summer evening, around eight o'clock. I am fourteen years old. Family friends have arrived. We sit out in the street, on our low brick front fence and on kitchen chairs brought out. An aunt asks for a cushion. An uncle lights a cigar. More people arrive. More chairs are brought out. We spill out into the street, across the pavement. My mother rushes about with cups of tea. My father whittles a wooden match and picks his teeth. Huge moths circle the streetlight outside our house.

Mr Ableman has just returned from New York and is telling us how it is there. None of us has ever been to New York. We listen attentively. "A ghetto," Mr Ableman says. "With my own eyes I saw things you wouldn't believe. The way people are living there, in holes in the ground. Not even in Poland, you didn't see such things."

Things have not been too good for Mr Ableman these past years. Three or four businesses. Nothing worked. He decided to try his fortune over there. "Land of opportunity," he said. "A new life." He had a brother in New York, a brother he hadn't seen for fourteen years. His brother would help him, show him the ropes. He sailed, leaving his wife and children, they were to come when he had it all right, and here he is again, less than a month later, flown back, sitting on our fence, a balding, clumsy man with large hands, telling us about New York.

"Even my brother," he says, "one room and a passage, that's all he's got. Maybe a kitchen. But a television? The biggest! My brother. Every night he falls to his knees and prays to God. But not for his wife, not for his children. You know what he prays for? For his boss. That his boss shouldn't die in the night, because then he'll lose his job. That's the life there in New York."

"*Schrecklich*!" cries an aunt, and the others quickly join in. What a babble. What a noise. Yiddish. Polish. A burst of Russian. I am embarrassed. What must our neighbours think of us, shouting in foreign languages, taking up half the street? I sit in the dark, ill at ease, looking at these wildly gesticulating people, these *Europeans*, these sudden strangers . . . and a dozen years later, in Lindos, it is exactly the same.

We are in a restaurant, just down from the *platia*, a dozen of us, drinking and talking. Someone has just arrived from London. He is telling us about the theatre, the new plays, about clothes, films, exhibitions, people. Everyone is shouting, questions, comments, laughing, and I sit there, feeling that same unease, wondering what the Greeks, the mostly silent Greeks at the tables all around us, are thinking. They are shopkeepers and labourers, the water man is here, three donkey boys, the postman, the plumber, and we are here because Greece is cheap. What it costs us a month here wouldn't last a week back home. And we don't speak Greek, maybe one or two words, because learning a new language is a strain and a bore, we've got better things to do, and anyhow, we get by. But I sit and feel uneasy and think, What do they think of us, drinking and laughing and shouting and not working in the middle of their village, in the middle of their lives? Do they like us? Do they care?

Four years later, one of us wrote a book about the expatriates of Lindos. It was a novel. It started with some kind of world-wide calamity that cut the island off from the rest of the world, and then went on to describe what the locals did with the writers and painters and poets whose outside money had been so suddenly cut off. They hunted them. They ate them. They put the girls into brothels. Finally they did away with the lot. The island wasn't named as Rhodes, but if you've ever been there, you'd know it at once. The atmosphere is exact.

A friend of mine tried it another way. He knew about expatriate colonies and he didn't want any of that. He rented a small house in an isolated village somewhere in Crete and every morning he worked in the fields with the farmers and labourers. He picked olives. He broke rocks. He learnt to speak Greek. He went to the local weddings and he drank in the local cafes and he lived on just the money that he earned. His thesis was that modern life had become frantic and he wanted to get back to basics. He lasted four months. Oh, the villagers were friendly enough, and he got to know some of them really well, but there was always a difference, a distance, a feeling of strain. "They couldn't understand me," he said. "Nothing was said, of course, but I could feel it there all the time. They thought I was mad."

Expatriatism. Expatriate. The very word. You think of Hemingway and Fitzgerald and all that Paris crowd. You think of Keats in Italy, Byron in Greece. You read about Henry Miller ferreting for crusts of bread in the cold cliffs of Montparnesse, and you know it must have been tough, but my, how romantic. You think, possibly, of Henry James, accepting all those dinner invitations in London, and writing in quiet Rye, those long, complex sentences, those subtle thoughts. You think of Joyce in far-off Trieste, reduced to giving lessons at Berlitz, labouring to unravel *Finnegan's Wake*. You think of Gauguin, that prince of expatriates, who fled his stockbroker existence, painting out his heart in primitive Tahiti.

But Gauguin hated Tahiti and spent most of his time trying to get back to France. Henry Miller doesn't live in Paris today. And Hemingway left, and so did Fitzgerald and Dos Passos and all the rest of that crowd. I don't know about Henry James. I see him as a satellite, forever in orbit, a cold observer, never really at home wherever he lived, the first mid-Atlantic man. James Joyce to me was a true expatriate, his mind never out of Ireland, his body unable to go back. But why doesn't Joyce's expatriatism have the romantic cloud of, say, Hemingway's?

And what a romantic cloud. No one wants to know about Gauguin's endless squabbles with the Tahitian officials, no one reads the dismal letters he wrote to his wife. We read Somerset Maugham's *The Moon and Sixpence,* the fairy tale version of the facts. The Paris of the twenties was a place of giants, of course, but how many of those giants would have come if Paris hadn't been so cheap?

But being an expatriate now, today, how is that? You sit in your room in Paris or in London or in Tangier or in Greece. You have your habits and routines. You work, or try to work. You go to restaurants for your meals. You have a drink at a bar. Your shirts are washed by a fatima or in a laundromat. You go to a movie. You go to see friends, if you have any. You go back to your room. Are you a romantic figure? Do people see you the way they see Byron and Keats and Gauguin and all those famous expatriates?

The people in whose midst you're living certainly don't. If you're lucky, they ignore you. Stay around long enough and they might even take you for granted, but always with certain reservations, subtle barriers, invisible walls. You'll always be somehow different. If you're a lone expatriate, your chances are better. If you're one of a colony or crowd, or even if you just have one or two similarly expatriate friends, the barriers will be higher. You could be resented. You could be disliked. Whatever happens, no one is going to see you bathed in any kind of romantic cloud.

But get a letter from home, from an old friend, say, and there it is, that cloud, that mythical light. Maybe not quite of Gauguin proportions, but there, unmistakably there. No real news, the letter will say, everything's much the same, but look at you, you lucky dog. The more mean your circumstances, the harder that light will shine through. And for a minute or two, you might even see yourself as your friend sees you, a romantic exile, making great sacrifices of your art. You could at such moments even think of going back. The Returned Expatriate, with attendant glory. Except then you'll stop being an expatriate. You brood for a long moment. You remember certain things. You frown. Enough of that. You answer the letter politely (no real news, everything's much the same), and then go back to your habits and routines.

A definition. What I think an expatriate is.

An expatriate is not an *emigre,* he is not an immigrant, he is not a refugee. His exile is self-imposed. No external forces or events make him quit the land where he was born. It is an inner thing. And whatever this inner thing is, it is such that he can't operate, work, live at home. He has to go. This is not to say that he will be happier where he goes. Happiness hasn't got anything to do with it. What is happiness, anyhow?

There are short-term expatriates. That Paris crowd. There are expatriates by default. I have a friend who has lived in London for twenty years. He went there initially just for six weeks, a holiday, was offered a great job, and the six weeks grew into two years and then into twenty. He says there's nothing all that special about London and there was certainly no reason why he left Australia. He's got used to it. Coming back is a matter of organization, finding another job, details. He's probably there for good. I don't see him as a true expatriate, not the way I define the term. A true expatriate, in Thomas Wolfe's words, is someone who can never go home again.

But you can try.

Somewhere during my expatriate years, I realized I had a secret card up my sleeve, and then I saw that all my expatriate friends had the same card too. And when things got tough, in Rome or in London or wherever we happened to be, we would sneak out this card and look at it, but individually, stealthily, each person at his own card, privately, unobserved. The card would warm us, comfort us, reassure us, and then we would slip the card back up our sleeve and put up with the toughness of Rome or the nastiness of London. This card was our most prized possession, we held it tight and close, never speaking about it, never showing it around. The name of this card was Returning, Birthplace, Home. It was there for emergencies. The final emergency. It could, you see, only be used once. After that, there was nothing.

I bumped into an Australian friend in London. He told me he was bored. I could see him looking at his secret card over and over, and finally he used it. He was back in London in a month. "I couldn't stand it," he told me. "It was all just the same, the same as it was when I left, nothing changed. I felt terrible, that old hemmed-in feeling, couldn't work, couldn't think. Well, London might be boring, but at least I don't feel that over here. I can work."

His secret card has gone. Now he is a true expatriate. The last I heard he was in America. I don't know what he's doing there. I don't know how he feels.

But I don't want you to think that for nine expatriate years I was a wanderer, a drifter, rootless and vague, roaming from country to country, from room to room. There was that, there were three years of that, but that was enough. I married. An English girl. We lived in a flat in London. In summer, aeroplanes flew over our garden and in winter the trees were bare and neighbourhood windows crowded in. A son. We took him to Holland Park, to the Kensington Gardens, to the Round Pound. He was too small for boats, but he watched, and also the men and boys flying their kites. I worked in an attic with a view of the sky, and through a window opposite and slightly below, a man with a walrus moustache sat at a typewriter, doing what I was doing, writing a book. We kept regular hours, made friends, paid our bills. But a city is a poor place to test your expatriatism, everyone is a stranger in a city, in a sense, and anyhow I hadn't been an expatriate all that long.

And then we moved out to the country, an old house on a hill. Our nearest neighbour was an ex-army man with a cherry-red face and an upswept moustache, the foreigner's exact image of a countrified Englishman. Tweeds, pipes, white pigeons. We rented this house for six months, and then we bought a house in a village about five miles away, a village with a church and a duck pond and quaintly thatched cottages around the village green. Here, for the first time, I put down real roots. My wandering days, I told myself, were over.

The village years. Quickly. Hollywood style. Pages falling from calendars like autumn leaves, fading scenes in fast montage, the writer at his table. "Morning," says the postman. "Morning," says the owner of the village shop. "Evening," says Mr Davies, handing me a Guinness at the Red Lion. Dominoes, smoke. Type, type, type. A brand new daughter. New ducks on the pond. Friends come up from London. "God, you're lucky," they say. Apple trees in the garden. The village fete. Type, type, type. And London, as the years go by, each time noisier and dirtier and more impossible to move in. The writer grows a beard. Daffodils, tulips, birds on the lawn. "Well, who would have thought I was the country type?" I say. Flip, flip, type, type. The reasons mellow and fall, and then advance again. Peace.

My wife announces she is bored.

She is too young, she says, for this country life. She misses people. She wants to be near the theatre, galleries, movies, shops. London is out of the question. She talks about Oxford. We look at properties. A suitable house comes up for sale. I go to the auction. The bidding soars over my figure in less than a minute and I am disappointed, of course, but also relieved. Why? And if not Oxford, then where? We talk about Greece, Portugal, moving to Spain, France. We spend hours and hours poring over newspapers, the letterbox is filled with leaflets from agents. Alone, I stare at maps of Europe, maps of the world. Where? I feel small and vulnerable, homeless and unwanted, adrift on the face of the earth.

The telephone rings.

It is Melbourne, Australia. My brother. Excited. He is getting married. "Listen," he says, "I know this is asking a lot, but is there any chance you can come over?" My reply is immediate. "I'll be there," I tell him. "I'll be there."

How right we were not to move to Oxford. I knew it in my bones all along. I am awake the rest of the night, staring up at the ceiling, on which is printed, in the open at last, my secret card.

Expatriatism is a sad and unnatural condition. I came back from Australia, my brother's wedding witnessed and celebrated, everything in order. A giddy month, gone in a flash. It was freezing. I walked around the village sporting a flashy tan. First thing after Christmas we put our house up for sale.

Agents. Tickets. Removal vans. We went to stay with an old friend of mine for a final weekend. I'll call this friend Roger Brown.

Roger has done well. He lives in an elegant house in the heart of the heart of the country, seventeen acres of woods and lawns, strutting peacocks, a man-made lake. He has lived in England for ten years.

He was surprised I was going back to Australia. "Why?" he said. "I thought you were nicely settled." I tried to explain it to him. I said I was a bit bored with England, but it wasn't just that. Going back to Australia, I said, just seemed the right thing to do. I ventured the opinion that expatriatism was a sad and unnatural condition, and if you could go back, you should. Roger exploded.

"Nonsense!" he cried. "Nothing sad about it at all. It's a perfectly natural process. It's like leaving your parents' home when you grow up. Perfectly normal. Never heard such nonsense. Have a whiskey."

But Roger has his suits made in Savile Row, his hair cut at Trumpers, he belongs to a select London Club. He has played billiards with Sir Ralph Richardson, he has a Purdy shotgun, he sits at a Sheraton desk. Over the years his voice has got slower and deeper, all trace of accent gone. He has become more British than the British, as they say, and if that's not unnatural, what is?

A few days before we left, I dropped in on that other friend, the one who has lived in England for twenty years. I told him I was going. "Good move," he said. "Australia is a great place. I might even see you there." "Could you really go back?" I asked him. "I love England," he said. "I'd miss it if I went back. But I miss Australia too. It's a strange business. When you become an expatriate, you end up not really living anywhere. Twenty years here and I still have an outside view of the place. Which, mind you, I quite like. Gives me a perspective. But you're right, it is an unnatural condition. In many ways, a bit sad. I think you're doing a wise thing going back. Good luck to you."

What else can I tell you? It's dark now. I have filled my room with paper and smoke and talk. From the window there is now no view at all. It's time to go home.

Home. What a strange and curious feeling. When I first got back and walked down the streets, streets I have known most of my life (the buildings have here and there changed, but they're only a veneer), I wanted to stop people and explain the situation. "I look ordinary," I wanted to say, "but don't be fooled. I am a returned expatriate. I have been away for nine years. I've just got back." But I couldn't, I didn't, what I was feeling was a private matter, of no interest to anyone else. I had lost a certain uniqueness, and I wasn't sure I liked that. Anyhow, it passed.

But something else has come, a different feeling. I walk down a street now, any street, and I feel something I never felt in Europe, never once in all those years, and I understand now about expatriates, why they club together and why they talk so much about the politics of the country they're in, why they are so strong in their opinions, the way they never were at home. The defence mechanisms. The cocoons. The resentment. The barriers. As I walk I know I have had returned to me something precious and essential, a thing beyond all measure, that thing which expatriates must always lack, and which they know they lack but can't do anything about, no matter how hard they try, and here it is, without my having to ask for it or do anything to earn it, automatically and naturally mine. A sense of community.

I never did go to Bialystock, the city where my parents were born, or anywhere in Poland for that matter. I knew there was no point. That world has gone. If my mother taught me nothing else, she taught me that. And my father's history, my father's past? I went to Israel. I was there a month. I walked around Jerusalem with one of my father's old friends, a limping, white-haired man who had hewn rocks with my father in the quarry. "This street," he said to me, "this street where you are standing. Your father and I built it." He knelt down and showed me the marks my father's chisel had made. "From here to here," he said, showing me the extent of his work. "He laid all this." I looked where he pointed. I felt excited, thrilled. "Look!" he said to a passing woman, grabbing her sleeve. "This boy's father made this road, where you are walking now." She looked at me. She looked down the road. "So?" she said, shaking her arm free. "It's old already. We need a new one."

NOTHING MATTERS

Exiled Author Shoots For The Moon

The most famous living resident in the charming English village where we make our home is a bushy-tailed grey fox who, last year (a typical year), spared my local innkeeper's twenty-four chickens the sorrows and trials of old age. Call me an impudent upstart, rank opportunist or starry-eyed dreamer, but this year I decided to wrest the crown of glory from his head.

Well, the decision wasn't exactly all mine. A certain nameless person had a slight hand in the business.

"Come out of that cupboard!" the good wife greeted me one frosty morning last month. "The time has come!"

"Just a minute, sweetie pie," I mumbled, frantically shovelling old shoes over the seventy-nine collector's item back issues of *Hoary Beaver, Swedish Spasm* and *Deep Inside Thigh* I keep in there for purposes of insulation and muscular control. "You spoke, my dear?" I inquired, coming out backwards like a chimney sweep's brush.

"O.K., so you're a shoe fetishist," said the good wife. "Big deal. Listen, I'm changing husbands."

I slumped to the floor, smitten by visions of the good wife's dowry whipped away, leaving me thin and penniless in the arms of a dozen girls of former acquaintance. The bouncy Barbara. The peerless Monica! Crazy, crazy, Yvette!

"I am tired," said the good wife, ignoring my spinning orbs, "of being married to a meek voice whispering in the wilderness. I have decided to link my name to that of a towering star."

"Nabokov?" I whispered. "Solzhenitsvn? Germaine (gulp Greer?

"Don't think I didn't write to them," said the good wife. "However, enough about me. From now on, it's all you. The time has come," she said, throwing me a suspicious-looking Kleenex, "to awaken this sleepy hamlet to the fact that in its midst resides a creative giant of no mean repute. Not to mince words," she continued, "when your new book comes out next week, this village will *know*!"

But I've already told the rubbishman," I lisped.

"Well, that's a beginning," said the good wife, snapping on her false eyelashes. "Get your clothes on," she commanded me. "In about seven seconds our babysitter, who is also the ace reporter for the local gazette, is coming around to interview you. Better put on a girdle, there's a photographer coming too."

"Hi," said our babysitter, exactly seven seconds later. "I wish I could interview you, but I can't spell. How about if you write the interview yourself and I just collect the fee?"

"Which one is Mr. Lurie?" said the photographer, peering through milk bottle spectacles at my collection of famous war criminals.

After they had gone. I lay on my hammock in the attic and considered the whole question of fame.

When I first came to this village, I caused to be posted a small sign on the notice board at the local newsagents. *World famous author,* it read, *seeks quiet barn in which to write Peruvian water ballet and other major works. Central heating not essential but don't be shy.* I sat back, waiting to be inundated with fabulous offers. Three weeks passed. Not a peep. Not a dog kennel. Not even a chicken coop. When I walked down the street, people shook their heads and went "Tsk tsk."

I decided to shame them into action, and for two months I wrote at a table in the front room, where passersby could see me through the plate-glass window, my brow tortured, steam rising from my fingers as I hammered out poems, essays and philosophical texts, the children gnawing at my ankles and the good wife in tears.

Still nothing.

And then one morning I found a note pushed under the door. *"Draw your curtains!"* it said. *"Have you no sense of common decency?"* It was signed, *"A Well Wisher."*

That did it. Sparing no expense, I moved to a friend's cottage three miles away, and though I found his whiskey watery and his champagne not of the highest vintage, there I stayed. When people asked me what I did for a living, I told them I was in Ferment.

"Wake up!" shouted the good wife, disturbing my attic ruminations, "there's another ace reporter on the phone."

Well, fame is a giddy thing, and before I knew what was happening, I found myself on page 11, sandwiched between a used car and a child molester.

Literary Lion, squeaked the headline.

When I walked down the street, people looked the other way.

"Graham Greene wasn't built in a day," the good wife told me soothingly. "Anyhow, it's all arranged for next Saturday. There's a poster going up near the sewage works, and the funeral parlor has promised to give you some space too. You're reading your new book at the local children's bookshop. How do you feel?"

"Fame doesn't frighten me," I said, running a comb through my eyebrows and beard.

Promptly at three on Saturday afternoon, I strode into the children's bookshop, cape swirling, a modest blush to my cheeks. The place was empty.

"I'm afraid we've clashed with an exhibition of modern fertilizers," the owner of the shop said. "Hold on, here come some people."

In slunk five whey-faced children, obviously all sent by a mother whose marriage was floundering, skin packing up, and — last straw — now the TV had given up the ghost.

"The Twenty-Seventh Annual African Hippopotamus Race!" I thundered, before they could make their escape, in a voice such as to make Richard Burton seriously consider another profession. "Once upon a time . . ."

An hour later, my voice worn to a frazzle, I woke the children and crawled over to the owner.

"Congratulations!" he shouted. "I've just sold a copy of your book!"

"For cash?" I croaked.

"Oops, sorry," he said. "Made a mistake. Wasn't your book

107

after all. It was the *Guiness Book of Records*. Which is selling very well, by the way. Can I interest you in a copy?"

But my little jaunt into the heady stratosphere of fame has had some effect. I can't slip into the local newsagent's any more and peruse the dirty books, as was my want. Everyone knows who I am now. They'll tell the good wife.

Family Circus

Because I have been such a good boy all week (I only fell out of bed three times, and the second time it wasn't completely my fault), the good wife says I'm allowed to go to the circus.

Not only that, but my four-year-old son consents to tear himself away from the telly for a few minutes (we've got him down to a basic eleven hours viewing a day, which might sound cruel to you, but we know what we're doing), and cross me over the street.

"Clowns!" I cry. "Acrobats! Incredibly sexy girls doing reckless things in fiendishly-abbreviated costumes on the trapeze! Let's go!"

"Steady on, dad," says my infant son. "It's only a small family circus, such as tours the villages and small towns of rural England, playing here a night, there a night, forever moving on. Don't expect too much. It's not like what you see on the telly."

"Are you crazy?" I tell him. "Why, circuses are the very stuff of life, incorporating, as they do, theatre, magic, the triumph of mind over matter, devilishly-skilled routines lovingly handed down from father to son, and don't forget the fiendishly-abbreviated costumes. Now, help me on with my astrakhan coat, we're going to be late."

I should note here that I never went to circuses as a boy. This is because my grandfather, who was in charge of me, claimed they were dirty.

"Feh!" he used to scoff. "If you want to step in things, do it at home."

He wasn't joking. One of the most embarrassing moments in

109

my entire so-far life was coming home from school one day with a friend and seeing my grandfather, who bore a curious resemblance to Sigmund Freud, dressed in his neat three-piece grey-striped suit (with the cufflinks, with the watch chain) standing in the middle of the road shovelling horse manure into a suitcase to put on his radishes.

The real reason he wouldn't take me to the circus, I see now, was the frustration he would have felt seeing all that prize elephant stuff going to waste. He was not a strong man, and could never have carried four full suitcases home.

Excuse me, I digress.

The circus (*Weights Family Circus, Fun For Young And Old*) has been set up in the field behind the library, and despite rain and a howling wind (it's spring in the U.K.), I note that quite a few fathers and mothers are in attendance, each chaperoned by a child.

"Curb your excitement," I say to my boy, who has plunked a paper bag over his head and is counting backwards from two thousand, "we're going in."

We seat ourselves on a suppository-inducing wooden bench and wait for the festivities to commence.

"Welcome, boys and girls!" cries a woman (who bears a striking likeness to the hard-eyed shrew who took my admission money) wearing a top hat and a black cutaway suit and stepping nimbly (considering her age and weight) into the ring. "We're going to have some real fun, aren't we, boys and girls?"

"Yes!" screams everyone except my television-trained son.

"And here comes the clowns!"

What a marvellous simulation of idiocy! The two clowns slouch around the ring a couple of times, mumbling things which I don't hear but which are no doubt madly humorous, and then one of them hoists himself up a three-foot ladder and begins to walk along a wire, a full dizzy thirty inches off the ground.

"See that?" I say to my boy. "No safety net. How's that for death-defying skill?"

He does this for twenty minutes, and then out comes a girl in a fiendishly-abbreviated costume who, without further ado, climbs a rope and hangs upside down for a while, flexing her muscles, doing a slow spin, and not once losing the rhythm of the gum-chewing trick she's doing at the same time.

"I want to go home," says my boy.

"Relax, kid," I say to him. "You haven't seen nothing yet. Look, here comes a pony. Now you'll see some tricks."

The pony is led on by a man who cunningly simulates Boer War veteranship, and who tells us, in a high falsetto voice, that the pony has been trained, no expense spared, to guess the ages of volunteer children from the audience.

Four children are instantly pushed forward by their parents, the talented pony tapping out their ages with a hoof.

"Bravo!" I shout. "Encore!"

"But he got them all wrong, dad," my son whines.

"A technicality," I explain. "He tapped, didn't he? What more do you want?"

"Interval!" cries the top-hatted woman. "Refreshments available in the foyer!"

There isn't actually any foyer, but a section of the tent is quickly set up for the sale of soggy crisps and cans of Coke, the goods dispensed by the abbreviated-costume-trapeze-spinner's absolute twin.

"Enjoy, enjoy!" I say to my son, handing him three crisps. "You're at the circus!"

After interval, some real thrills!

An American Indian (who curiously resembles the wire walking clown) strides three times around the ring going "Ho!" and "Hoy!" and then spits fire from his mouth.

"Big deal," says my finicky son. "The kid next door can do that."

Then out comes a bear who walks on a barrel, assisted only by the top-hatted woman who grips its nose and the Boer War veteran who stands behind it with a stick giving skilful bum prods at crucial moments.

Finally, the trapeze girl comes back, this time spinning anticlockwise on her rope, no easy feat.

"Can we go home now?" says my son. "I'll never make up the stuff I've missed on the telly."

"You have just witnessed one of the great features of English life!" I shout. "The travelling family circus! Men might have gone to the moon but the circus lives on forever!"

"Look out dad," says my son. "You're stepping in the elephants."

111

The Quest For Top Loonie

The subject is oddballs, loonies, weirdoes and freaks, the out-of-kilt and out-of-step and out of the whole deck of cards, the slightly warped people (assuming that the rest of us are straight), the eccentrics, the unclassifiable, the almost bizarre, also, perhaps, yes, why not, that certain showbiz element, for this is New York, after all, and what's New York if not showbiz?

(If it makes you happier, I am typing this with my knees.)

But let me do this, straightaway, before this discussion gets underway, let me make some attempt at definition, at delineation:

I am *not* talking about the mumblers, the lip movers, the funny walkers (unless they combine this with some other great thing), nor am I talking about the blank-eyed starers into space, the long-distance sitters, the human statues, for this, as I've said, is New York, and New York does these things to a person. I mean, I did some mumbling myself today, also some funny walking and staring into space, and before I knew it I was walking up 43rd Street and going up in an elevator and into an office . . . hey, I'm in the wrong office! wrong day! wrong time! wrong person!

Come in anyhow, they said. Rest your eyeballs. You see. They *know*.

No, what I *am* talking about is . . . and there's no other word for it . . . is . . . or should that be are? . . . the *brave*.

Here comes the first one, right out of my window. Black, bearded, wearing a kind of coolie straw hat, an old guy, walking slowly down the street, not looking at anyone or anything in particular . . . and singing the blues at the top of his voice. Shouting. Real hollerin' going on there. He does this about once a week, usually on Sunday round ten in the morning, makes his way up this end of West End Avenue, out onto Broadway, hollerin' the blues in that crazy coolie hat. But mark this, because this is what I'm talking about, this is the whole thing: He's not begging, not panhandling, not out for the tourist trade. Hell, he just loves to holler the blues.

Down near 42nd Street, just off Times Square, we meet our second loonie, right out in the street, traffic zipping past on both sides, and he's sort of bent over in an unbelievable crouch, and what he's doing is . . . *playing the street*. I mean, he's got a pair of drum sticks and he's doing taps and bounces and rim-shots and all manner of fancy stuff, a regular Gene Krupa of the bitumen, and he's not begging either, he hasn't got his hand out . . . I mean, how could he? . . . but there's no hat for you to throw pennies in either. He's just getting off his own private show right there in the middle of the street, is what he's doing.

Loonies, loonies . . . they're all over the place. There's another drummer too, except this one plays a real drum, and boy does he play it bad . . . hammers it, bangs it to death . . . really thunders, incredible brio . . .

Enough about drummers and hollerers, let's get into the hard stuff, the real performers, and I guess the best (so far) has to be the guy I saw this morning, on the subway, on my way to talk to a top literary agent, and I mean so top even the clouds look up, so naturally I'm nicely dressed and possessed of a certain reserve and I have all the necessary documents and etc all clasped tightly to my body and I'm sitting there on the train which is zipping along like a jet-propelled pneumatic drill under the surface of Manhattan . . . and suddenly I hear this whistling and then a figure rushes into the compartment . . .

I'm dead, good-bye . . .

It's this guy in a kind of silky Superman suit, except the trousers part is shorts, a black guy, with one of those afros not yet totally out of control, and look, he's wearing roller skates! and he's got this whistle in his mouth, like an old postman's whistle, and he's blowing as he skates! and there he goes in a flash of silk, cape flying, whistle blowing, zooming into the compartment and then out the other end, Jesus, he's doing the entire train, one end to the other! and he's a nimble bugger, I'll tell you that, you can't imagine how he gets around people, doesn't bump into a single one, all he does when his speed needs to be put under a certain control is grab hold of one of the shiny metal stanchions or poles and gives himself a sort of spin, once around, twice, and then off he goes, out the door, out of my life . . . gone.

Whoops, but I left out, neglected to mention . . . in his left hand he's holding, carrying, . . . a *briefcase*! The kind of briefcase you see up and down Madison Ave, as toted by top execs . . . and I go into this fantasy where I imagine he's New York's top stockbroker rushing to Wall Street to buy cheap and sell dear . . . important man . . . definitely a loonie . . . but sharp, shrewd . . .

I ascend in the elevator to the premises of this lofty literary agent, heart beating, and not just from the altitude . . . and out she comes to greet me . . . My God, she's all blotchy orange! Like her makeup was put on in the dark . . . by a practical joker spastic . . .

To hide my shakiness I tell her about Superman on rollerskates with the briefcase. She listens, her face, under the blotchy orange, perfectly blank.

"Last Tuesday night," she says, when I have ground to a silence, "I went out to catch a cab and all of a sudden I heard this voice behind me . . . 'Want to share a cab?' . . . and I turned around and it was a gorilla . . . well, he was going in the opposite direction, as it turned out, so that was that . . . and then two days later I saw another gorilla, a different gorilla, running for a crosstown bus."

"Cigarette?" I say.

"No thanks," she says, doing something to her ears. "I'm trying to give them up. As a matter of fact, I've had staples inserted in my ears . . . you don't know about staples? You want to look at them? Well, I don't blame you. I try not to look at them myself. What they are is, well, if someone offers you a cigarette, you press each staple for about thirty seconds and it does this thing in your head and after that you don't want a cigarette . . . hey, where you going?"

Where I am going is Central Park to check out if the man and the girl all dressed in purple including purple sunglasses and a purple rinse through the hair sitting on purple bicycles when they're not scooping up horse manure into purple sacks are still there. I saw them last year, but I guess they've moved on. Purple was last year. You can't hang around in just purple. The competition is too stiff.

115

The Truman Capote Guide To Genuine Real Friendship

I have always liked Truman Capote. Admired him immensely. Hell, *worship* isn't too strong a word, is it? I mean, the guy is small and bald and fat and he's got this curiously high pitched voice such as to affect the bladder of a bat, but has that stopped him? No sir. Tru is tops. You'd have to look for at least seven seconds before you could find a guy with *half* Tru's gumption and spunk.

I mean, how many writers do you know prepared to hang around the Death House in Kansas City for eight years, just to talk to a couple of miserable killers, with no other reward at the end of it all but your photograph on the cover of *Newsweek* and *Time,* apartments and houses in five major world cities, and an intro to hobnob with the celebrated jet set?

Would Faulkner have done it? Hemingway? Erika Jong?

No sir, Tru is top of the tree, and we should fall to our knees and praise the lord on high for the privilege of being able to suck in breath concurrently with such a giant.

As a matter of fact. I have just fallen to my knees. I am sick, man, very sick. An absolute killer virus has taken up residency in my frail body (four rooms, share kitchen and bath), but never fear, I am fighting back. I am ingesting such vast quantities of Vitamin C that before you can hum the complete works of Sibelius, I will be cured.

Meanwhile, while the noble fight rages within my dainty frame (dirt floors, but nicely raked) I am using my spare time wisely. I'm not just lying about. No, sir. I'll tell you what I'm doing. I'm reading *The Daily Telegraph Magazine,* which comes to me each week not only airmail from the Mother Country but rolled up so tight it takes me three weeks to flatten out the little bugger, much less read the immortal prose within.

But it's worth it. I mean, this week there's a nice piece about how unfair death duties are, especially if you're rich, and then a really thrilling piece about how the wine-growers of the Champagne district now have their own airline, and after that, for those who can take the pace, there's a blood-racing assessment of NATO, complete with smudgy photographs and intricate maps. This *Telegraph Magazine* really is something else, what?

Then there's a piece about yachts and the men who sail them, and then, just when you think you can't take any more, it's a cardiac arrest for sure, what should look out at you but a photograph of — gasp! — boys, it's Truman Capote!

Yep, it's the littler battler himself, and you know what he's doing? He's *interviewing* himself! Well, when you're an artist of Tru's stature, you don't take chances with semi-literate hacks, do you? No, sir. I mean, they might ask you the wrong questions, for God's sake. Or cadge a cigarette off you. Or even *vomit* on your cashmere vest, you know how those semi-literate hacks are, faced with a real giant.

O.K., I'm cutting the preamble, I'm getting to the nitty gritty at last. Tru asks himself how it is to be rich, and he says it's all right, and then he slips out the following: "I know very well a considerable number of very rich people (I don't count anyone rich who can't quite quickly summon up 50 million dollars in hard currency)."

Now, I know I don't have even one teensy weensy bit of Tru's boss talent, but no one likes to feel that his friends are all paupers and knaves. So this is what I do. I mean, my sanity is at stake, not to mention my standing in the community. I summon up all my friends, and as each one comes in the door, I request him nicely to empty his pockets, just to reassure myself that I'm not associating with bums.

First in the door is my old pal the ex-expatriate eleventh rate designer, the little Max. He comes in encrusted with Yves St Laurant pendants and if he hasn't got 50 mill on him, I'll seriously consider becoming the dentist my dear mother always secretly hoped.

118

"Unload those pockets, the little Max," I tell him. "This is a test."

"I haven't got any pockets," he says. "This is a Paco Rabane fiendishly innovative one-piece knitted suit and you ought to see the performance when I have to do something basic like take a crap. I'm lucky to be alive, what with these cruel winds of winter playing about my body and all."

"No 50 million!" I wail. "Next!"

It's the great Rappaport, top thief in the antiques business, also spiffy dresser and gifted mumbling raconteur.

"Unload the pockets!" I bark.

Out comes a Louis XVI Kleenex, a length of Ming Dynasty dental floss, and a fly button from Julius Caesar's second-best toga. Ah, but he's a crafty devil, is the great Rappaport, much too wise to walk around with all his baskets in the one egg.

"What's in your shoe?" I ask.

"My foot, man," he replies.

"Truman Capote, have mercy on my soul!" I wail, falling to my nose. "O.K., one last chance. Next!"

In leaps the great Dr Nameless, who is not only one of your very top psychiatrists, but practically a personal friend as well. His Mickey Mouse T-shirt heaves with authority as he dances into the room, eyes ablaze as he ferrets through my cupboards for a smokable cigar.

"Dr Nameless," I entreat him. "I am desperate for a peep into your pocket, where I know, let's face it, there's 50 mill for sure."

"A loonie!" he cries, whipping on a mask of Sigmund Freud and jumping up onto my stereo. "I'm the one who asks for 50 million around here. I mean, I'm a doctor, you're nothing but a quack. Quack quack! Polly want a biscuit? You're all crackers, you're all trying to drive me mad! Look, I'm having a heart attack on the premises and I'm not even charging you!"

The last I see of the great Dr Nameless is the sweat on his back as he bicycles wildly down the street.

Oh Truman, forgive me, I have failed. Paupers and bums are my lot, and the least I can do is cart out the rubbish before my wife gets back. And just in time too, here comes the rubbish truck.

Hey, and look who's driving! It's Aristotle Onassis, in actual person, gripping the wheel.

119

All of which might sound a trifle farfetched to you, but you haven't got thirty-seven million grams of Vitamin C coursing through your body. I mean, last week I saw the King of Spain. And I'm not telling you what he had in his pocket.

Proust Sinks Choppers Into Yiddish Onion Roll

Once a week I set off in search of the past. Leaving the good wife to do her best in the bathroom (where she's lavish with my costly after shave, but what the hell), I herd the kids out to our second-hand 1964 EH Holden Special, the windscreen wiper knob of which is held on with spit, and the same goes for the rest of the mighty vehicle, but until my Maserati comes from England this will have to do.

It's Sunday morning, about quarter to nine, the streets of Melbourne all peaceful and quiet except for the howling and whining of my kids. I look around frantically for my paperback Dr Spock with which to give them a slight censorious tap about the dandruff.

Don't hit us, father!" they wail. "You'll only cripple yourself with guilt and spend endless hours tossing and turning on your narrow bed, reviewing your shoddy life and wondering where you went wrong."

"True enough," I say. "But what would you suggest?"

"Bribes!" they cry. "Quieten us with bribes!" Silence our mouths with chocolate sailors. Also comics, plastic ray guns, sickly licorice, and I don't even think we'd say no to a nice wedge of apple strudel (the super sweet) with a bucket of rich cream on top and a side helping of chips."

"Jee — zuz!" I howl. "I'm trying to set off in search of the past and you're talking chocolate sailors. Where did I go wrong?"

"O.K., daddy," they say, knowing full well that with tears in my eyes I'm liable to crash the car, "we'll be good. Tell us once again about your hangups while we sit here like angels and digest your every word."

So as we roll gently down Punt Road (I've left the car in the garage and we're going by barrel instead), I begin to intone the story I tell them every Sunday morning, after we've got the howling over and the business of the bribes.

"Once upon a time," I begin, "there was this weedy little Frenchman named Marcel Proust —"

"Ban the bomb!" shout the kids. "Halt the Pacific tests! Boycott the frog bastards until the camembert grows out of their eyes!"

"Ssh, kids, let me finish. This Marcel Proust one day, having nothing better to do, dropped a hunk of cake into his tea, and the second the oozy mess hit his gums he was flung into such a deep remembrance of things past that twelve volumes (in French) were to elapse before he could ever drink tea again."

"Dig that crazy prose style," wails one of my kids, rolling his eyeballs to and fro.

"Ssh!" I snap. "I'm getting to the good part. I am, as you know, a recently returned expatriate, and once a week I tool gently down to St Kilda, gums at the ready. Yep, kids, it's Acland Street for me, the good old Village Belle, where the 'cakes may be sickly and the women who sells them are all ravishing beauties to a man, but Acland Street is the home of (gulp) the sacred — Onion Roll!"

"Whoo whoo!" sing the kids.

"Now, children," I counsel them, "there are two kinds of onion roll, and I'd better tell you what's what. First, there's the *soft* onion roll, which is absolutely delicious, easy to butter, and slips down the throat a real treat. You can eat ten of them in a row and still ask for more. Beware of this onion roll! It's a phony! This is your *upstart* onion roll, a recent invention made for God only knows what ulterior motive (but I suspect for money), and to be shunned like the very pox. I shudder at its very mention. Your *real* onion roll, children, the genuine article, is the other, which I will now describe."

"We feel sick," says the angel kids, but I choose to ignore the little beasts. I'm getting to the good part, no stopping me now.

122

"Imagine, if you can," I say, "a small platter of concrete with an aftertaste of rusty tin. On top is a liberal lacing of real onion which on a clear day with a powerful electron microscope practically leaps to the eye. Got it? Now try to butter it. Instantly all the onion falls off, also the poppyseed, setting you back five bucks at the dry cleaners. Now, place the sacred onion roll in your mouth. What happens?"

"Your teeth crack," the kids whip in.

"Only if you've got teeth!" I cry, my dander up. God, these modern children. Don't they understand anything?

"Kids," I explain, "you're not getting the total picture. What happens, you see, when the sacred onion roll hits the gums, is that you've instantly flooded with a remembrance of onion rolls past, twelve volumes (in broken Yiddish) of how my mum used to bring them home in the old days and we'd sit around the kitchen table with our sophisticated power tools remembering how they used to do it in Bialystock (Poland) with mules and ropes, the local rabbi occasionally leaping in and attempting to rend the rolls asunder with the cutting edge of a wise old Biblical saying, and a wonderful time was had by all."

"We're desperate for chocolate sailors," the children weep.

Well, how can you explain it to them? What would they understand? Have they ever experienced true suffering, or anyway being breathed on by a religious person? Nothing, the little innocents!

Hey, look, we're in Acland Street at last, and just in time too. There's the bakery van, the chap's swinging open the back doors now, and if I rush I'll have first squeeze.

"Wait here, kids!" I cry. "Behave yourselves and chocolate sailors will rain down on your heads like warts! I'm off!"

Money changes hands, onion rolls are flung into a bag, also a plentitude of those damn sailors, and at three hundred miles an hour (or its secondhand 1964 EH Holden Special equivalent) we rush back to the flat.

"Stand back, kids!" I command, seated at the kitchen table. "The sacred onion roll is only inches from the mouth and in about three seconds I am going to be flooded with such a monumental remembrance of my lousy childhood that it's probably safer if you went into another room. Here I go!"

Crack!

"Oh dear," say the kids. "Daddy's done it again. Anyone here got a remembrance of good Yiddish dentists?"

Fiddlers Under The Roof

Word has just reached us of an incredible burglary, beside which the legendary rifling of Brinks fades to total insignificance. This burglary happened to a friend so naturally we can't mention any names, but what happened, see, was that these burglars got into this house in Albert Park (Victoria, Australia), where, spurning the diamonds, bars of gold and Mickey Mouse ticklers everywhere strewn about, they descended like vultures (if you'll pardon the coining of yet another immortal simile) upon a medium-priced stereo and five hundred long-playing records. So what's incredible about that? Wait a minute, wait a minute. There were *more* than five hundred records there, but these burglars didn't want them all. No, sir. These were your discriminating burglars, such as Cary Grant would certainly play in the movie of the same name if he wasn't so crippled with money. What they did, these burglars, was methodically go through the pile and whenever they came upon a folk-singer — whoosh! — into the fireplace it went. Joan Baez? Out! Lightnin' Hopkins? Bang! Sonny Terry and Brownie Magee? A pox upon them both! Bach they took, Miles Davis ditto, even Mario Lanza, but let their beady little eyes fall upon a Muddy Waters or a Memphis Slim or a Champion Jack Dupree — whoosh! out! feh! What a pair of truly discerning musical burglars, we thought, the instant we heard the news, and immediately tried to contact David Williamson (the beacon in the night of new Australian playwrights) thinking this was material right up his alley to turn into yet another box office bonanza, but the great David, his answering service lisped at us, was out having his hair lengthened and couldn't be disturbed. Henrik Ibsen and

125

William Shakespeare were similarly engaged, so, in desperation, we put words to secretary ourselves. Steel yourselves, boys, the curtain's about to go up and we don't want any Jaffas (the wonderful chocolate confection with the orange centre) rolling around during the serious parts.

Scene: The front room of the home of a friend's friend's friend in Albert Park (Victoria, Australia). Diamonds, bars of gold and Mickey Mouse ticklers are everywhere strewn about. As the curtain goes up, enter two burglars, SULLIVAN and SCHMOCKMEISTER, both wearing trousers featuring capacious pockets, also masks, beards, noses and legs. It is Sunday afternoon, about five o'clock. The place is as quiet as only Albert Park (Victoria, Australia) can be on a Sunday afternoon around five.

SULLIVAN: Hey, dig the loot! Diamonds! Bars of gold! Mickey Mouse ticklers even! Wheeeee!

SCHMOCKMEISTER: Vot's de matter vid you, Sullivan? Bars of gold? Vot are you, some kind of heathen *ganef?* Dig de stereo already! Dig dose discs!

SULLIVAN: Stereo? Discs?

SCHMOCKMEISTER: Ah, de voild of music! Vell do I remember de days in Bialystock (Poland, Europe) ven ve used to sit around the samovar eating day-old bagels and drinking reconditioned tea mit outside de Cossaks beating on de door and making all kinds of pogroms in de snow. De poverty! De suffering! But did ve care? Not vun bit! And let me tell you vy not! Becoz in our hearts voz music! In our hearts voz Bach, voz Mendelsohn even and already! In our hearts voz maybe too ve become great concert pianists and fiddlers and all det stuff and bring a little happiness to de voild, a little culture, to say nothing of getting out of de foul ghetto. Sullivan, please be so kind to slip dot stereo into mine left-side capacious pocket.

SULLIVAN: My first real job and what do I get? A musical loonie.

SCHMOCKMEISTER: Enuff mit de small talk. Give me de discs. Vait! Vot's det? Big Bill Broonzy singing "Throw your mamma dem underpants, I done hoed me a weary row and I wanna go home"? Feh! Reminds me of de ghetto.

126

SULLIVAN: Boss, boss! Do my ears deceive me or is that a police siren wailing ever closer and closer? Let's get outta here!

SCHMOCKMEISTER: Muddy Waters singing "Ole man river comin' up mah cistern, flushin' away mah beans and grits"? Double feh!

SULLIVAN: Boss! We ain't got time to sort out discs! Let's just grab the lot and run!

SCHMOCKMEISTER: Hokay, hokay, don't make a panic, I'm coming. Joan Baez? *Doopeh!* She hasn't even got big tits. Vell, not a bad haul, let's go home.

(Exit SULLIVAN and SCHMOCKMEISTER, the latter humming Yiddish melodies as he steps over the sill. Almost at once the door bursts open and in flies GEORGE MUSICLOVER, followed by his wife MOZARTELLE.)

GEORGE: Good God! Either we've been burgled or the cleaning lady came a day early!

MOZARTELLE: And look what crazy burglars they were. Not a single folksinger did they take.

GEORGE: Aha! Is that so? Well, I've got a surprise for them, whoever they are. Last night, you see, I had a curious dream about a pair of burglars named Sullivan and Schmockmeister breaking into our house and taking the medium-priced stereo and absolutely every single disc that didn't feature a folksinger, so you know what I did, dearie? This morning, before you were up, I came down and changed all the sleeves.

MOZARTELLE: You mean — ?

GEORGE: That's right. The second they attempt to slip some Bach on the medium-priced stereo, you know what they'll get? Mississippi Slim howling out, "I got warts all over my body, baby, but I still shave my legs for you."

MOZARTELLE: Well, every cloud has a silver lining (to coin yet another immortal simile) and here comes yours.

(MOZARTELLE picks up a handy bust of early-period Bob Dylan and stoves in GEORGE's cranium, as the curtain slowly descends.)

A Short History Of The Jewish Barbecue

WELCOME TO YOUR ADVENTURE IN OUTDOOR LIV-
ING! whispers the box within lies my recently purchased
firemen's-red-clip-on-windguard-wind-up-handle-foldaway-legs-15-
inch-portable barbecue (tongs extra). I assemble it in the living
room of my modest Australian suburban home. It looks beautiful.
There it stands, on the lush floral carpet, flanked to left and right
by massive stereo speakers and my priceless collection of grimac-
ing Winston Churchill toby mugs (definite Battle of the Blitz
ambience in every sip of cocoa), sweetly singing its message of the
great outdoors. I am so moved I vacuum the mothballs off my pith
helmet and ferret frantically in the fridge for an ounce and a half
of vital quinine.

It runs in the family, this love of the great outside. Why, did not
my very grandmother, about whom I will not have a word said,
not only replace her lawn with *green* concrete, but on warm days
stand outside with a hose and give it a drink?

My favourite uncle is a keen outdoors man too. For at least ten
minutes a year (or even longer if he falls asleep), he sits outside
on the imitation-marble patio of his skilfully designed home unit,
enthroned on plastic and chrome, exhaust fumes from the busy
road only three feet away protecting him from poisonous butter-
flies and murderous birds, running his eyes gratefully over the
rocks, gravel, concrete and sand that constitute his slice of God's
domain. Why, with my own eyes I have seen him kick back a
small stone that has errantly strayed from its rightful place. There's
a frontiersman for you. There's a pioneer of the wild outside.

But the subject is barbecues, their upkeep and breeding and

role in a happy marriage, and my fierce love of them, Doctor, dates, I suppose, from that day when I was twelve and saw my mother running outside with a frying pan that had caught fire. It was a nervy performance and no mistake, the flames definitely no laughing matter but my mother, lack of eyebrows notwithstanding, attempting a nonchalance so as not to shame herself before the prying eyes of our goyishe neighbours. And when I came to sample the sculptored anchovy she had miraculously wrought from the pound and a half of best steak in her pan — man, I was hooked.

Comes now the expatriate years, exiled in wintry England. Lonely and alone, I wandered the streets of London, not exactly sure what my life lacked, but something, something . . . when suddenly I spied, right in the middle of Leicester Square, your great Australian outdoor barbecue, in actual action! I sped forward, aided by dogs' droppings, but what was this? Where sizzling steaks should have lain in state, or anyway top quality chops and a plentiful handful of bangers, a blackened Englishman was barbecuing . . . measly chestnuts. However, one must make allowances for the singularities of national identity, and I crowded close in my bulky Acrilan coat (indistinguishable from fur at only two thousand paces) and whispered to the vendor, "One bag, please."

And as he scooped the charred roundies into a little English bag, why, I felt within me a keen awakening of all things Australian. My eyes stung with memories. Smoky visions crowded my brain. And that smell! I ransacked my past, trying to place it. The Richmond football ground's men's toilets at three-quarter time? The inside of my gladstone bag when I had been forced to take a *pesach* lunch? That nice man I once met outside the Princess Theatre when they were doing Puss in Boots? No, not quite, not exactly . . . and then I happened to glance down.

"Hot shit!" I screamed. "My coat's on fire!"

"No extra charge, luv," snapped the vendor, moving like lightning to save my wallet from possible harm.

Years passed. Children accrued. Happiness poured like rain onto my expatriate head. There wasn't a thing that the good land of England could bestow that I didn't possess, or anyway have in hock. Outwardly I was calm and at peace, the very model of streamlined evolution, but inside was a different story. Charred chops! Burnt bangers! Singed steaks! A remembrance of things barbecued burned within me like a secret lust. But whenever I mentioned this secret lust to my secretly glorious English wife, she claimed it was constipation and doled out a suitable powder.

But truth will out, and one day I found I couldn't restrain myself a moment longer, quickly fashioned an altar of bricks and slates and on top the grill from our gas stove, and everything was going nicely and even my wife was moderately impressed and we spoke of emigrating when suddenly the sardine slipped down through the grill never to be seen again and we had to patch up the marriage with Ritz crackers and Horlicks.

Ah, memories, memories, and here it is Sunday lunchtime and I'm trundling the brand-new barbecue out into the garden. Charcoal is unobtainable, owing, said the man in the woodyard, to recent heavy rain, and the same goes for red gum chips, so it's heat beads and metholated spirits, a sight to warm the heart of any I.R.A. man. Also the smell does wonders for the palate.

"Wait till you sink your choppers into this," I advise my jostling brood. "It's your absolute essence of the entire Australian outdoors in every single bite."

I build it up nicely, pour on the meths, throw in a match and — ah, here's a bonus, away goes all that unnecessary hair on my arms. "Do it again, pops!" scream the kids. My wife books passage back to the U.K. "Happy Yom Kippur!" I cry, hurling on the steaks.

In less time than it takes for a rock to melt in your mouth, the things are done and done. Gingerly, tenderly, proudly, I hand the first steak to my six-year-old son. Poor little blighter. Born and bred in poverty-locked England, let him taste at last the truly great things in life. "Here you are, boy," I say, tears of tenderness welling in my eyes. "Your first outdoor Australian barbecued steak experience."

His little milk tooth sinks into the hallowed meat. His infant jaws take up the slack. And then — what? he hurls the meat across the garden, with incredible Zen accuracy hitting the neighbour's cat smack in the very face.

"I've told you," says the darling English angel, stamping his tiny little foot. "I don't like meat done in a disgusting way!"

Sunday

Whoops, it's Dr Nameless! Emerging from his aubergine Porsche bearing fresh bagels and cream cheese and lox and sometimes a *challeh* (the semi-sweet) and certainly a container apiece of gefilte fish and chopped herring, occasionally also a container of a special sort of spicy cheese spread which I don't know the name of, I always order it by pointing, plus, in the other hand, Jewish versions of Cheese Danishes and Apple Danishes, these dainty confections of a size such as even cut into quarters it's a recklessness not to have an iron lung close to hand.

Is the coffee ready, the orange juice?

Good! Let's eat!

This is every *second* Sunday I'm talking about here, this Yiddish stuff for breakfast, though the Doctor comes every week, has been for years, it's a ritual, it's the nice thing we do. On alternate Days of Rest it's my turn to lay on the eats, and what I plump for are croissants and brioche and *pain chocolat*, also not neglecting, if they've got them, those special brioche things curled round and around and then held together with a mortar of custardy creamy stuff, juicy raisins studded aplenty all over so you can be sure you're getting your ample Vitamin C.

Fresh. I'm talking fresh. Out of the oven fifteen minutes ago, twenty minutes if I've had to stop for lights. Listen, I drive fourteen miles for this top stuff, seven there, seven back, distance means nothing when you're hooked on comestibles of this calibre.

O.K. We're eating, we're eating. A nice breakfast.

Jesus, look at the mess!

This Dr Nameless, I should tell you, is a top psychiatrist, an incredibly learned man, why, there's scarcely a paperback on the subject he hasn't skimmed, and while we're eating — and his speed with the gefilte fish is a whole other thing — he is chastizing me on the upbringing of my children, he is telling me that behind every father there is a mother, except in the case of his mother, behind whom there is nothing, his is the last word in mothers such as you wouldn't believe, all this while I am slicing the bagels and making nice sandwiches with the cream cheese and the lox such as I didn't learn how to do from my parsimonious mother, God rest her flinty soul, and I'm pouring out the coffee nicely and making sure everybody has got a clean plate, and now he is telling me that my neatness is a symptom of something maybe very serious, look at the way I'm rushing in with the vacuum cleaner just because of a few crumbs on the carpet — a few crumbs? it's an entire bakery down there! — and then, having delivered himself of all this, he either swipes one of my Dunhill cheroots or produces one of his Ramon Alloneses (the monster big) and proceeds to stink up the place something dreadful while I'm trying to have a nice eat.

My children are lying on the floor, woozy with multiple quarter sections of the Apple and the Cheese.

My English wife is picking at her gefilte fish in a goyishe manner.

I have risen from the table and am playing loud jazz.

The Doctor likes gutsy stuff. If it's Les McCann he's happy. The minute I put on intellectual stuff (Miles Davis) he's out the door.

So am I. Eleven o'clock already. Time to work.

I drive to my room. This is ten minutes away, in the house of an elderly albeit incredibly spritely couple — Mrs Anonymous is eighty-six, her husband is eighty-eight — who, even though I've been coming here for three years, still think that what I do for a living is scrunch up perfectly-good paper to put in the waste-paper basket so Mrs Anonymous can take it out every afternoon and burn it under the copper to warm her bones.

Also I pace a lot, which is my way of keeping warm.

Now. The first thing that happens, when I come in the door, tumultuous with breakfast — either the Yiddish or the French, the effect is the same — is that Mrs Anonymous presents me with a cup of tea, also, unless I'm lightning quick, either a plate of biscuits and cheese or a cardiac-sized wedge of her own home-made apple cake with fistfuls of cinnamon sprinkled nonchalantly on top.

"Mrs Anonymous," I say, showing the whites of my eyes, also lifting up my jumper to give her a peep, "I am close to death with eating."

Mrs Anonymous clicks her tongue, convinced I am fading to nothing before her very eyes, but I am not having further food.

"One biscuit?" she says hopefully. "How can you drink tea without even one little biscuit?"

"Nope."

I sit at my table, light a cigarette, wind paper into the type-writer, work for an hour or two on my Nobel Acceptance Speech or any other small matter I have at hand, not forgetting, from time to time, to scrunch up the odd sheet to keep Mrs Anonymous happy, all this while odours of roasting pork, baking potatoes, mashed pumpkin and scrumptious apple pie tiptoe from the kitchen under my door and into my consciousness.

Mrs Anonymous is making lunch.

My God, I'm starving to pieces here!

What's the time?

I drive home in an absolute froth of malnutrition.

Funny business, these wives. Sunday lunch is either the total gravy roast such as is learnt at the mother's knee in distant England and keeps dry-cleaners in profit, or it's the table randomly pockmarked with those items from the fridge that, to quote herself, "need eating." An ankle of month-old cheese. A goitre of salami. The suspicious bit of the beetroot no one wanted to touch all through February. Stuff like that. I don't know, there's no pattern to it, a man doesn't know which gastric juices to have in readiness as he comes through the door.

Whatever.

We eat.

Now follows the crucial time, the actual marrow of this terrible bone called Sunday.

In a word: What to do?

Rake leaves, paint the fence, chop wood, oil the mower, fix the son's bike where the handlebars have gone all wonky and the kid's going to kill himself seriously one of these days, or, worse, the damn bike will fall over and scratch the garage door?

Naah.

Don't want to do jobs.

Jobs is not for Sunday.

Writers, you have to understand — and I'm talking serious writers here, not your "Oh what a nice hobby, let me show you *my* poems" writing folk — don't do jobs on Sunday because they can do jobs any old day of the week, in between novels, for instance, when they're waiting for the wells of inspiration to refill, also in between chapters, when there's nothing like oiling a mower to let the subconscious work on that tricky part just coming up where you're trying to decide should you let the heroine stay a virgin until Chapter Two, or, what the hell, give her the business right on the opening page.

O.K. no jobs.

What then?

You can't go for a drive because everyone is doing that and anyhow, where is there to go?

You can't go to the Cultural Centre because that's too depressing. All those kids sliding on the parquet floors.

There's nothing in town.

You can't drop in on people because they'll just be sitting around in the same despair you're in and you'll only increase your own looking at them.

What?

Got it!

The afternoon sleep!

From which I wake up in desperate need of a cup of coffee and a slice of chocolate cake, only I've got to be careful here, it might be too close to dinner, and then it depends which dinner, is it the gravy roast as is learnt in England at the mother's knee which the wife neglected to serve for lunch, or is it the "needs eating" stuff which still needs eating, in fact, even more desperately than before.

I have a whiskey.

A second whiskey.

I listen to noisy jazz.

Ah, It's dinner.

We're eating.

What's on TV? There's nothing on TV.

Read a book. Have another whiskey. Stare into space. From

136

time to time sneaking peeps at the watch to see is it . . .

It's ten o'clock! Made it! Bed time!

We read, cosy as toast on the electric blanket turned up to number three. We make ourselves drowsy with words. We turn out the light. We make, if we're feeling that way, the beast with two delicatessans. We drift into sleep.

Good-bye Sunday . . .

Except nine times out of ten I wake up, and so does the wife, truth to tell neither of us has been really asleep, we've just been pretending.

The thing is . . . we're hungry!

Starving!

So either I get up or the wife gets up and whichever one it is makes the nice tea in the nice mugs and brings it in with the plates with what's left over from the nice breakfast with the Doctor, and all around it's peaceful and quiet as awful Sunday slips away for another week, this time as almost every time, around the sound of our zestful chomping.

I'm Gonna Sit Right Down And Write Myself A Letter

You step into a restaurant, *the* restaurant, the one all the top gossip columns have said is the place to be, to be seen in, where it's impossible for ordinary people to get in. "Ah, Mr Raymond!" cries the head waiter, bowing to the floor, kissing you on both cheeks, fondling the hem of your garb, and all those things waiters do with such style if you're the right person. "Your table is ready, Mr Raymond!" he booms, ushering you in with a swoop and a sweep past the astounded gaze of your betters to left and right.

Very nice, what?

Except your name isn't Mr Raymond.

That dumb waiter, despite many rehearsals and I don't know how much in bribes, has got it wrong.

Never mind.

Try again.

You engage (at staggering cost) a cluster of giggling albeit shapely-legged schoolgirls to descend like vultures upon you on the steps of the London Palladium at six o'clock on a Tuesday evening, furnish them with autograph books and small scissors (large scissors can be dangerous), and at six on the dot you step out of a cab, plenty of ink in the gold Parker pen you have borrowed from a friend for the occasion, your hair grown long so that souvenir locks may be taken aplenty, and — but what's this?

Just at the moment an Actual Real Famous Person steps out of another cab, it's a Marx Brother! it's the Duke of Edinburgh, it's —

Done again.

Oh, Fame, where is thy sting?

Or, to put it another way, does one (me) have to shuffle through life unregarded and unapplauded, a (gasp) Total Unknown?

Of course not.

One (me) is not a creative giant for nothing, after all, and so here's what I do.

I push a crayon into the hand of my good wife, lock her into the downstairs loo, where there's plenty of paper, and cry as follows:

"Fan mail, good wife! What greater index of Fame is there than fan mail! Slip 'em out under the door as they come, my dear, I'll be ready!"

And while the good wife scribbles, I pluck a quill from a nearby turkey, check that my inkpot is full, and —

Ah, here comes the first one.

Dear Mr Lurie. I work the hose at the local abattoirs, my husband is a model of piglike bestiality, my best friend (Zelda Kopp) has given me a rash, and if it wasn't for your celestial prose, I think I'd shoot myself. Bless you. Yours truthfully, Phoebe Raghorn (Mrs).

Dear Mrs Raghorn, I'd like four pounds of sausages (mixed), a side of lamb, and a bag (if it's no trouble) of giblets. Regards to your husband. Oink oink.

Dear Mr Lurie, I have just finished your "War and Peace" and wonder if you're writing a new one at the moment. Keep up the good work. Yours ever, Freida Chekhov (Miss, alas).

My dear Miss Chekhov (alas), Last night a frog got into my bed, but every frog has a silver belly (to coin a phrase), and there suddenly came to me, whilst standing in my torn and tangled sheets, a wonderful idea for a new book. It's about a train driver who runs over a commuter (Anna Karenin, a foreigner) and misses his connection with the 8:04 to Banbury, the 9:26 to Paddington, and his tea break at Elephant and Castle. His ex-wife returns home just so she can leave him again, his teenage son takes up tattooing, and he starts to go (naturally) to pieces. I haven't quite worked out what happens next, but I'm spreading my sheets with frog food and negotiating seven figure (two of them big ones) paperback right. Stay tuned!

Dear Mr Lurie, Spellbound reader of your every magic word though I am, I can't help wondering why you never write about possibly the most wonderful of England's many blessings — her beautiful wildflowers and natural beasts (moles, snipe etc). Yours hopefully, Alastair Philpott (Mrs).

Dear Mrs Philpott (or whoever you are — as if I didn't know), Do I tell you what to do? Do I meddle in your life? When you began to eat bootpolish sandwiches, did I say a word? A peep? A whisper? A hint? If you want to besmirch your face with left-over lard (amongst other things), that's your business. If I want to sneak around Soho in my dirty rubber raincoat (causing no harm to any human being), that's mine. Live and let live, O.K.? Please remember me to your dear mother.

Dear Morry, Long time no see! When are ya coming back? I've got thirty-seven million tubes of the good stuff in readiness inside the fridge, plus several gallons of the vintage hard stuff hidden under my bed in the sleepout — get the message? Give us a tingle the sec you land — fair enuff? Bazza.

Dear Bazza (?), I think you've mistaken me for some other chap. Partial though I am to a fine dry Chablis with my oysters in the morning, I don't understand what you mean by "tubes" or "good stuff" or "sleepout". And the only Bazza I know (or knew) is Roderick McBazzerington-Smythe, whom I met briefly at Gstaad in the winter of '49. But thank you for your interest, I'm sure.

Dear Mr Lurie, You don't know me, but my name is Cynthia Meadows, I am nineteen years old, interested in Ecology, Ancient Egyptian Art, and Modern Dance, and at the moment I am writing a thesis (for my Master's Degree) on the Genius, Wit and General Brilliance of Morris Lurie. My father is a multi-millionaire and I will be in London next week. I hope you don't mind me writing to you like this, and taking up your valuable and precious time, but the thing is, I don't know a single person in London, and I wonder if it's all possible for you to meet me at London Airport (or wherever's convenient), because I'd really like to talk to you for a few minutes. Just so you'll recognize me, I'm five feet two with eyes of blue, my general measurements are 38-24-36, and I will be wearing a pink orchid in my windtossed hair, and a deep dimple in my left buttock. Please come! Yours, Cynthia.

Dear Miss Meadows, I have a wife, two children, a mortgage and a cat. I am respected in the village where I live, and am on nodding terms with the vicar and the milkman. However, in the interests of Modern Literature, I can manage Thursday afternoons and alternate Tuesdays. I don't want to appear nit-picky, but could you send me a photograph of your person in leotards or bikini (or whatever) just to keep me going till Thursday. I append a box number and remain faithfully yours. P.S. If this is my brother playing one of lamentable jokes, I am not fooled.

Dear Mr Lurie, On behalf of the Nobel Peace Committee, I have great pleasure in informing you that the Nobel Prize for Literature has this year been awarded to you. The voting was unanimous, each Member speaking highly of your rugged style, human compassion, and singular and poetic grace, to say nothing of your life-long struggle for Good against Evil and the betterment of Mankind. Trusting this meets with your approval, I have enclosed a stamped addressed envelope for your speedy reply. Yours most humbly, The King of Sweden.

Dear King, Thanks.